S0-BKR-501

TWO CULTURES *of* BELIEF

The Fallacy of Christian Certitude
A Systems Approach

RONALD QUILLO

TRIUMPH™ BOOKS
Liguori, Missouri

Allen County Public Library
900 Webster Street
PO Box 2270
Fort Wayne, IN 46801-2270

Published by Triumph™ Books
Liguori, Missouri
An Imprint of Liguori Publications

Scripture quotations are taken from the *New Revised Standard Version Bible,* Copyright © 1989 by the Division of Christian Education of the National Council of the Churches of Christ in the U.S.A. Used by permission. All rights reserved.

Library of Congress Cataloging-in-Publication Data

Quillo, Ronald.
    Two cultures of belief : the fallacy of Christian certitude : a systems approach / Ronald Quillo.
      p.   cm.
    Includes bibliographical references and index.
    ISBN 0-89243-819-3
      1. Christianity—Essence, genius, nature. 2. Bible—Hermeneutics. 3. Faith. 4. Certainty. 5. Modernist-fundamentalist controversy.
I. Title.
BT6.Q55   1995
273'.9—dc20   95-12690

All rights reserved. No part of this publication may be reproduced, stored in a retrieval system, or transmitted in any form or by any means—electronic, mechanical, photocopy, recording, or any other—except for brief quotations in printed reviews, without the prior permission of the publisher.

Copyright © 1995 by Ronald Quillo
Printed in the United States of America
9 8 7 6 5 4 3 2
First printing

REA

ALLEN COUNTY PUBLIC LIBRARY
L

3 1833 02863 4076

273.9 Q4t
Quillo, Ronald
Two cultures of belief

ALLEN COUNTY PUBLIC LIBRARY
FORT WAYNE, INDIANA 46802

You may return this book to any location of
the Allen County Public Library.

DEMCO

For
My Colleagues, Friends, Associates, and
Students
at
Oblate School of Theology
San Antonio, Texas

Contents

List of Figures

Acknowledgment

Special thanks to project editor Anthony F. Chiffolo of Liguori Publications for his patience and professionalism in assisting me in the preparation of the final manuscript.

On Rivalry and Its Guises

The Peril of Labels

C onflict makes news. Headlines and sound-bites thrive on contrasts gleaned from the tumult of human interaction. If there is no tumult, if there is only marked discord, even if there is only calm but fervid disagreement, the well-turned phrase can give the appearance of tumult and so provoke an audience's rapt attention. Labels are applied, not indiscriminately perhaps, but often with an undaunted assumption that their meanings are fixed. *Conservative*, for example, boldly pits one faction against another marked by *liberal*. The penchant for such sensationalism could be ascribed to commercial interests. For the print, sound, and visual media are answerable to their markets, not only their respective markets, but to one another's markets as well.

The need to sell breeds competition. And competition too can be heralded as a form of conflict. The facility to draw boundaries, to breed factions, to establish parties is an aspect of human creativity and the enriching process of diversification. Conflict is diversification gone sour. Common goals and cooperation give way to one-track thinking and a desire for domination. The proclamation of conflict, whether by the media or anybody else, is symptomatic of a cultural condition. For such touting of discord is part of a social system, a circular system in which human differences and the naming of them have become mutually instigating. When conflict takes a specific form and appears to be inevitable, a culture—or, as is usually the case, a sub-culture—may begin to believe that only one side has the truth. Such belief can serve just causes. But it can also perpetuate destructive fallacies. Here an instructive label becomes a perilous epithet.

On the surface, *Two Cultures of Belief* is about little more than conflicting methods of biblical interpretation. The major parties or "cultures" are designated as fundamentalist and critical. Their rivalry is depicted as one that can either serve their common Christian interests or, without due care, deprive both methodologies of a wholesome larger vision. The issues are specific and purportedly internecine. But the analysis of them is systemic, delineating the contours of rivalry so that polarization can be seen as a servant of cooperation. In many situation, persons on both sides long for such solidarity even when labels forbid its appearance. From this perspective, reconciliation of these two cultures can serve as a paradigm for other kinds of peacemaking, whether by parties embroiled in disputes or by those who strive to facilitate accord without taking sides themselves.

Working for peace means facilitating change in hearts as well as cultures. For antagonism, where it takes hold, plagues both individuals and institutions. The peacemaker, who is often a diplomat, may try to impact all conflicting elements at the same pace. When that is not expedient, beginning with individuals will in many cases work as desirably as beginning with structures and institutions. For the discord is systemic, all of its elements being interrelated and mutually supporting. To impact one of them is thus by a ripple effect to impact them all. What is essential is to gain some practical entry into the system.

Help from Differing Helpers

Several years ago I suffered a personal loss. Until that point there were many things that I had accepted as given. Now I questioned them. As I tried to examine my beliefs, and to find ways to move beyond the pain, many people came to my assistance. Friends, acquaintances, relatives, fellow parishioners, colleagues, advisers, and even strangers provided comfort. For me, a somewhat independent and inward type, that was an unusual experience. But I felt an urgent need to be open with others. I experienced a certain drive to seek them out and to let them help me.

Much of our interaction touched on spiritual matters. After a very short time it became evident to me that persons of many different types were able to help. For that I could be grateful; the more who could help, the better. Religious preference seemed to have relatively little to do with anyone's ability to relate to me in some beneficial and loving way. Their particular religious views appeared hardly to affect the authenticity of the spiritual encouragement these people offered. For me, this was especially noticeable when persons drew on the Bible in quite distinguishable ways. Those who did so in a very fundamentalist way appeared as one extreme compared with those whose approach to the Bible seemed substantially less literal. And my own religious preferences and assumptions seemed hardly to affect my sense that someone from either persuasion was capable of truly assisting me. From each, in a different way, I was able to be helped by words that were personally meaningful and religiously inspiring.

A few years later, as part of a sabbatical project, I completed a unit of Clinical Pastoral Education in a general hospital. Again, I experienced religious preference and interpretation as matters of limited, nearly irrelevant moment in times of need. This time, however, I was a participant at the other end of care. As the only professor among talented pastors, chaplains, and seminarians of various religious persuasions, I too worked at improving my ability to support persons with various problems and at various levels of crisis. I learned how to be more effective as a minister. I also learned that the other ministers, no matter what their Christian denomination or what their approach to the Bible, were being likewise effective. And through all of this the religious preferences of the patients appeared to make little difference. Most were cordial and welcomed our ministry no matter what their religious background may have been.

How Much Difference Does Biblical Interpretation Make?

These experiences helped clarify for me two questions regarding Christian exegesis or biblical interpretation: At the level of religious faith and awareness, what is happening when differing views of the Bible cause significant divisions in Christian teaching and ministry? And conversely, what is happening when such differences among Christians scarcely disturb their mutual support and pursuit of common theological interests and pastoral goals?

As I wrestled with these questions and discussed my thoughts with my students, it became increasingly apparent to me how the matter of biblical interpretation could be provocatively considered in a way that could serve ecumenical interests. I found that my keenest insights came by considering scriptural interpretation—namely, any method of understanding the Bible—as part of the larger context of religious belief. I found, in other words, that biblical exegesis, as I proposed to investigate it, needed to be understood as part of a culture, as one element of an entire spectrum of beliefs and institutions that embody the particular ways whereby the Church carries out its mission in faith, hope, and love. I had sensed this in a vague way since my student days, and now this perception was upon me with vividness and urgency.

The insight was hardly novel with respect to claims regarding the contextual nature of knowledge. In laying out principles of interpretation, hermeneutics and other sciences had long been able to articulate interrelated factors involved in drawing conclusions. In its own way, and perhaps with less optimism regarding one's awareness of truth, deconstructionism pointed in a similar direction, arguing in part that expressions function meaningfully because of an accepted coherent context. They are thus relativized by or dependent on the various elements (language, thought patterns, symbols, and so on) of the context. Because of such dependence, what truth individual expression conveys is quite problematic. My own perspectives, however, appeared to be positive with regard to biblical faith. I found it gratifying that the conclusions I was drawing from this approach resonated among people with quite varying exegetical persuasions, that is, with quite different preferences regarding biblical interpretation. So-called liberals and so-called conservatives seemed now able to approach one another, bound together in new harmony without necessarily forgoing the original positions to which they felt the biblical word bound them. Such harmony did not always ensue, however, so I have not been allowed to suppose that I have come upon any final resolution to the problems posed by my questions.

From Systems of Strife to Systems of Peace

This book is an attempt to explain and substantiate my conclusions in terms of what I call exegetical rivalry. I am trying to show that various views of the Bible or various systems of interpreting it can become systems of conflict because of assumptions or conclusions that, as they appear to me, are questionable. I am, therefore, hoping to sketch out ways in which the biblical word can be accepted as part of systems of peace, as part of contexts in which varying interpretations can be recognized as helpful to unity and to Christianity's cause. Here, rivalry can become emulation. The book is thus aimed at anyone within a Christian context who may be seeking new avenues toward such accord. But insofar as *Two Cultures of Belief* provides a structured analysis of scriptural interpretation as part of a larger system of meaning, the book can also be helpful for any reader seeking further insight into the assumptions and processes inherent in various approaches to the Bible.

My presentation of the issues is interdisciplinary in that it draws on several areas of study, including system theory, theology, hermeneutics, psychology, and the philosophy of religion. While in each there are specialists accustomed to using the methodologies and theories of other disciplines, an appreciation of the interconnectedness of the various fields of learning is a notable feature of system theory (Davidson, 187). Having found the principles of this discipline to be particularly relevant for the matter at hand, I am thus offering a fresh perspective on exegetical rivalry and one that may help bring peace to an area of frequent strife.

I do not propose that this is the only avenue or even the best avenue to such peace. My approach invites the reader to consider the possible limits of his or her previous understanding of biblical interpretation. Such consideration could lead to change. This kind of change—whether it concerns the Bible or anything else—does not need to mean the abandonment of a preferred methodology, procedure, or way of life. The change may, however, involve appreciating such a preference in a new way so that the enduring truth of it might be more fully disclosed (Heidegger, 91). Newness of this kind can, in a context of conflict, generate either satisfying reconciliation or necessary retrenchment.

An Overview of *Two Cultures of Belief*

Chapter 1 presents the issues and defines the terms of the debate with the help of system theory. Chapter 2 sketches the main theological elements that pertain to the discussion as I see it. In chapter 3, I attempt to show the merit of various methods of biblical interpretation and at the same time to comment on the risks inherent in any of them when used in certain ways. With chapter 4, I offer a vision of a new context whereby exegetical rivalry might better serve the general interests of Christianity. Chapter 5 contains my suggestions for fostering this vision at various levels in the Church and academe or for different age groups. My reflections conclude with chapter 6, an extrapolation on the challenge of such a vision to numerous controversial issues other than biblical interpretation.

To facilitate the reading of the text, I have provided a list of definitions as an appendix.

TWO
CULTURES
of BELIEF

Chapter 1

The Problem

Current Study of the Bible

Academic Issues

The professor has begun an introductory course on Scripture. It is an elective, so the students are present under minimal constraint. Thus far they have been fascinated by the historical background of the sacred text. Intellectually curious and enthusiastic about the issues, they are examining the events and ideas that helped shape the text or influenced those of whom the text speaks. Under discussion may be Egyptian archaeology, Persian history, or Hellenistic philosophy. The students appreciate the advances in modern science and scholarship that help illuminate the scriptural author's vocabulary, concepts, and frames of reference. Some of the students may find the background of greater significance than others; the conversation is respectful of alternate views.

1

The atmosphere changes, however, as the professor begins to deal with the composition or writing of the text. He or she is explaining in light of some current scholarly theories how the text seems to have been put together in its present form, what notions of history likely influenced the authors or editors, what literary forms appear to have been used, what the overall plan and purpose of a given biblical book seems to be, what assumptions the author may have had about the hearers or readers of the text. It might be proposed that an author traditionally associated with a given biblical book is only an alleged author, that certain statements (for example, regarding animal life or the stars) are refutable in terms of modern empirical science, that certain stories traditionally thought to be historical are actually fictional, that the roles of men and women were determined by changing social structures, or that the deeds of certain biblical characters, including Jesus, may be exaggerated or even fabricated.

Disturbing Factors

Now, many of the students are uncomfortable. Some may feel that the truth of the Bible is being seriously questioned. Some may even feel that their very faith is being attacked. Several of them are shocked, angry, or defensive. A few challenge the professor to the point of disruption. Some of the students who are comfortable with what the professor is saying become irritated by the discomforted students. The irritation springs from a perception that the discomforted ones are being close-minded, unrealistic, or even naive; the irritated students may even wonder if there is a place for them in a community of believers in which this kind of discomfort at modern scholarship may predominate. In a heated discussion, each side tries to defend the correctness of its position. They seem to have reached an impasse.

More and Less Literal Interpretations

Grades of Literalism

Scenes like this are not uncommon and are played out in settings other than the college, university, or seminary. Increasingly, high school and adult-education courses—as well as sermons— contain evidence of the teacher's or preacher's sensitivity to certain claims regarding the impact of modern scholarship on biblical exegesis. Such sensitivity often represents a preference for a less literal rather than a more literal interpretation of the scriptural text. The expressions *more literal* and *less literal* are purposely used here to avoid a facile or clear-cut distinction between literal and figurative interpretations of the Bible.

Those interpretations called more literal are ones that appear rather unassuming regarding the objective correctness of most biblical statements presented as factual accounts or as moral directives. At issue, then, are perceived degrees of historicity regarding events and perceived degrees of normativeness regarding rules. Among those who prefer the more literal interpretations, exceptions are made for obvious stylistic forms such as allegory or parable or for texts that may otherwise be thought to have figurative or metaphorical meanings (Barr, *Fundamentalism*, 40-49). Clearly, David's reference to God as a "rock" (2 Samuel 22:3) is a poetic and theological flourish; and there is no need to insist that the "prodigal son" (Luke 15:13), as depicted by Jesus, actually existed. Common sense as well as a literary sense for imagery can thus guide literalists in a figurative interpretation of numerous biblical texts (Averill, 63). Moreover, texts regarded as prophetic are frequently interpreted, even by the literalist, according to their perceived symbolism rather than their literal meaning (Ammerman, 44-45).

The result is a variety of interpretations, even among those who generally lean toward literal meanings (Boone, 42–44). Moral directives are usually thought to pertain unambiguously to daily living (Ammerman, 7, 42, 52–54, 195, 200); but increasingly in recent years, through extended or metaphorical interpretations, such imperatives are also related to the political and social scenes as well (Ammerman, 202; Falwell, Dobson, and Hindson, 193–95). Those preferring more literal interpretations are thus not inflexible. They are often persuasive, however, and are exercising notable influence on public morality and policies (Neuhaus, 14–15, 19, 43).

Interpretations called less literal are those that in much greater measure allow for exceptions to literalness. Genesis 1 and 2 may be regarded as "mythical," namely as poetic or imaginative depictions of God's creative activity and power; whole biblical books, such as Jonah, may be taken as fictional; or certain acts of Jesus—such as his explicit claim, "Before Abraham was, I am" (John 8:58)—may be held to be unhistorical, though of great theological importance regarding Jesus' identity. Modern scholarship is allowed to work a philosophical, literary, or historical critique on the biblical message, to influence significantly the interpretation of the message, and in this sense to be critical.

The point of such methodology is not necessarily to deny the truth or credibility of the biblical passages, though historically the critical approach to the Bible has sometimes been used in this way (Wink, *Transformation*, 11). Rather, the intent is often to allow such passages to speak their truth through more literary forms than historical account or obvious nonhistorical forms such as parable (Soulen; Tate). The origin of the universe can by this approach still be regarded as God's doing even if the literal truth of the six days of creation is denied; God's call to Israel through the Jonah story to proclaim divine forgiveness to the Gentiles can remain imperative even if the story is thought to be fictitious; the status of Jesus Christ with respect to humanity and divinity can remain unchallenged even if the historical facticity of some of his statements is not acknowledged. Such an approach to scriptural texts often finds great resonance in academic circles and among those who enjoy mixing faith and science in such ways. Nonetheless, these less literal interpretations remain, for reasons to be suggested below, profoundly disturbing for those who prefer more literal approaches.

"Fundamentalist" and "Critical" Interpretations

The difference between a more literal and a less literal interpretation of the Bible can be called the difference between a fundamentalist approach and a critical approach. The term *fundamentalist* has a number of meanings (Falwell, Dobson, and Hindson, 2–4), as does the term *critical* (Keegan). In this book, these terms are being used as general designations referring to two divergent attitudes about the truth of biblical statements presented or appearing as factual or permanently normative and to two respective methods of interpreting these statements in the service of Christian faith.

The designations deny neither that some fundamentalist interpreters use certain critical methods nor that some critical interpreters adhere to certain assumptions in an uncritical way. In other words, the terms are functional and flexible, neither denying that fundamentalist interpreters may to varying degrees be critical nor that critical interpreters may be fundamentalist from certain perspectives. It is recognized here that within each group there is a spectrum of views, from conservative to liberal, regarding the degree of factual information or permanent truth in the Bible. It is also recognized that the scholarly study that has been used in conjunction with the fundamentalist approach has attained high respectability in academic circles (Noll, 8–9, 11–31, 72–141; Evans and Berent, 150–52), as has the learning used in support of the critical approach (Keegan; Tate). That either approach has become divisive is today beyond dispute. Tenacity regarding either leads to alienation between Christian denominations, rivalry between factions within denominations, or even disputes between Christians within the same local congregation. What from one perspective is at issue is the nature of biblical truth. The fundamentalist interpreter asserts that this truth, where accounts appearing as factual or normative are concerned, is communicated in essentially literal terms; the critical interpreter asserts that the truth of biblical accounts presented or appearing as factual or normative is communicated through a wide variety of literary forms (history, myth, legend, exhortation, proclamation, and so forth). From another perspective, or so it can be argued, the issue is how truth is claimed to be known through distinct forms of religiousness.

The Nature of Faith or Religiousness

A Unique Form of Awareness

Faith, or religiousness, can be called a form of perceived well-being by which persons say they enjoy a satisfying relationship with the divine. Believers or religious devotees typically claim to be aware—often intellectually, intuitively, and emotionally—that they rely on the divine for guidance and ultimate security. Depending on their religion or tradition, they may speak of their state in any number of ways—for example, as enlightenment, release, being born again, being in the state of grace, or being saved.

This awareness can be distinguished from forms of awareness such as empirical knowledge, logical inference, or interpersonal insights. Most sensory awareness seems undeniable because of the immediacy and clarity it appears to have—the air is hot or cold; I am inside or outside; the television is on or off—and it would take some doing to prove to me otherwise, to convince me that I am dreaming or being deceived. Traditional empirical science relies on such clarity in demonstrating through repeatable experiments the truth of its theories. The conclusions of logic have a similar power over the mind; when all the facts are in, the masterful sleuth can persuade even the initially incredulous that "the butler did it."

Though one is often on less solid ground with regard to the way people act or commonly relate to one another, the constants of human nature and the established patterns of relationships allow human beings to be understood and to enjoy a certain amount of predictability: the parent knows what pleases the child; one spouse knows what will rankle the other; the psychotherapist can predict a change if certain conditions prevail. In interpersonal matters there are variables that make inferences less reliable than those of sensory knowledge or logic. Persons are usually free to act unpredictably; individuality and human creativity in themselves prohibit casting persons into inflexible universal types (Jung, *Self*, 16–18). From the latter perspective, interpersonal knowledge can be said to resemble the peculiar nature of faith.

Faith may be regarded as awareness ultimately verifiable only within its own sphere and thus as something tenuous and demanding a good deal of trust. This can be seen both from the perspective of faith and at least partially from the perspective of the nonreligious forms of awareness just mentioned. By the terms sketched thus far, neither sensory experience nor the conclusions of logic can in themselves provide the evidence of the divine that faith or religiousness provides. And typically, the divine is not perceived to be present as fellow embodied human beings usually are. From the perspective of religiousness, the divine is present to someone whose personal openness permits a lively sensitivity to a dimension beyond that of everyday experience, to a transcendent domain that appears as the place of the sacred or holy. Thus in John's Gospel, Jesus can say that anyone who sees him through faith sees the Father (14:9–10). The divine or transcendent appears as something very real yet mysterious; it is accepted or believed in as that which is definitely disclosed yet partially remote and hidden. The realm of the divine, like the kingdom of heaven, is for those who have the eyes to see and the ears to hear; and these are not eyes and ears attuned to empirical reality alone.

Firmness in the Known and Unknown

From such perspectives, it is understandable that continued faith involves commitment, risk, and the pain of at least occasional misunderstanding and error. Augustine suggested that total comprehension of God is ignorance of God. Faith is guided by a divine light that always moves the commitment into the darkness of the unknown, a darkness that only further light and commitment can overcome. Here, religiousness bears a strong resemblance to deeper interpersonal relationships (Fowler and Keen, 18) such as those often existing between friends, married partners, or parents and children. Such relationships, though markedly experiential, involve the growing realization that the other person so deeply known is nonetheless unknown or mysterious. Thus, deep relationships must be ever-deepening, growing through ever-renewed and ever-renewing dedication and closeness.

Faith, then, involves mystery. At the same time, since the divine is known in faith as that which is ultimate or absolute, a sense of rightness and absolute firmness accompanies it. For a Christian, Jesus' word communicates truth itself. Within its own sphere, faith is sure of itself and its awareness in a way that parallels the limited kind of surety that can come even with empirical, logical, or interpersonal awareness. As a state of well-being, faith is typically more than knowing information and experiencing the relationship. It is typically, as well, a deeply satisfying stimulus and effect of all the believer's activity. This means that faith—like other relationships—can stimulate as well as be stimulated by certain stances or certain forms of action. Such is true of new faith as well as of renewed and growing faith. For example, faith can stimulate a believer's concern for the poor or it can emerge or be deepened as the result of a person's meaningful action on behalf of the poor. Meaningful action brings a sense of doing what is morally right, satisfying, and purposeful. A believer involved in meaningful action feels right in the world and can even feel a firm sense of destiny. Firmness of faith brings peace and joy.

Faith, then, is religiousness in which rightness can bring a sense of righteousness, and firmness can bring a sense of absolute meaning. Faith can be the unshakable foundation of one's ultimate peace, like a house built upon rock (Luke 6:48). This is true even when faith faces absurdity and tragedy. The believer may radically question life's meaning yet continue to trust and go on. Faith can prevail even when it is defied. And this is possible only if there is still some meaning. A mother may tragically lose her child because of a drunken driver; her faith can help her find meaning even if the death of the child seems meaningless. So the power of faith is often experienced as absolute.

Faith's Relationship to a System

Elements of a Setting

Faith, though ultimately a relationship with what is experienced as the divine, is born and perdures through a variety of closely related elements. Images, concepts, feelings, activities, objects, and social structures coalesce to form a context that both expresses religiousness and shapes it, giving it specificity. Such elements are the means of believing in a certain way, as a Jew, Christian, Hindu, or Buddhist, for example. This context also serves as a medium by which the divine is sensed or known.

Even as we can know people deeply yet depend on their behavior, body language, and words to know them, so must most believers depend on relevant means of knowing the divine, particularly when this knowledge prevails in association with a given religion. Images and concepts constitute the messages of the religion with which the faith is associated. These teachings may also be spoken of as the religion's content, which may be provided by the sacred writings of the religion and/or by the teachers or leaders of the religion. In either case, these images and concepts are accepted by the devotees and influence their religiousness. The content becomes a collection of ideas about the divine to which believers relate in a deeply personal way. They may, for example, associate the divine with a certain symbol, such as a bird, or may imagine the divine as an avatar, the divine in a human form; or they may think that the divine has no relationship to time and is thus eternal.

From this faith there typically emerge certain feelings. The affectivity of faith can take various forms, including satisfaction, delight, responsibility, and thankfulness; or the devotees may primarily feel that the divine should be feared or loved. Such feelings are often the prime instigators of activity on the part of believers. Such activity, which may involve the use of certain revered religious objects like candles or totems, may be individual or social and have to do with a variety of aims, among which typically are worship and service to others. If the activity is communal in nature, it will usually require structures or groupings; these too may be means through which the believers feel close to the divine. Such structuring ordinarily gives rise to leaders. And it is the leaders of a religion who often provide or expound the religion's content. The circularity of this arrangement of elements is sketched in figure A. It illustrates the "feedback" (Bertalanffy, 41–46) that takes place within the system of elements with which faith is involved. The system constitutes a kind of culture, or at least a subculture.

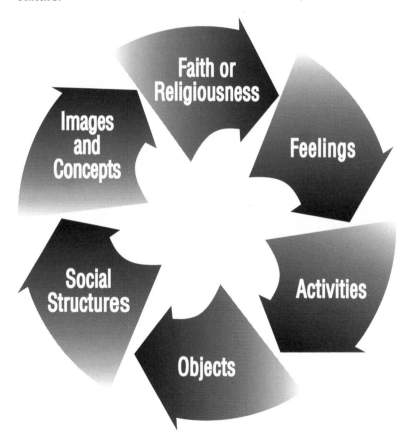

Figure A. The Circular Context of Faith

These elements can be further explained in terms of Christianity alone. Christians live their faith by speaking of God in a certain way, often with the help of biblical images (such as "spouse" or "judge") or in association with the figure of Jesus Christ. They may conceptualize their relationship to God in terms of forgiveness or grace. Certain feelings like remorse, joy, or thankfulness may be common among them. Typically, they will use objects such as Bibles, bread, or banners to engage in formal worship, or will behave according to certain ethical norms. And for most of them, certain leaders or ministers enjoy positions of prominence. These are but a few of the multitudinous elements categorized as images, concepts, feelings, activities, and social structures that coalesce to constitute Christianity as a religion.

Actually, the relationship of these elements as here illustrated is much more complex (Lines, 150–51) since each of them can directly influence all the others, not merely the element to its left on the chart. For example, the devotees' images and concepts can directly affect how they feel or act, relate to others, or fashion objects of art: from the religious notion of obedience there may ensue feelings of dependence, acts of submission, and respect for the lines of authority.

Systems and Subsystems—Settings Within Settings

In system theory (a science devoted to the understanding of the organized, interrelated, and/or organic structure of reality or life at all levels), such a broad and complex, but organic or self-conditioning coalescence of elements (Bertalanffy, 55; Lines, 44) can be called a general system. One of the best examples of such a system is a living organism, for the life form and all its parts cohere in "total reciprocity," namely as mutually conditioning one another (Davidson, 81). But systems can be found in all areas—including the material, psychological, social, and cosmic, as well as the biological—and at every level, from subatomic elements to the astronomical universe (Laszlo, 29, 177–78). Various factors—including temperament, training, and cultural influence—induce us to look at many things or individuals as though they can essentially be understood in isolation from their environments. A systems approach, which looks at all matters ecologically or with consideration of their relationships to the surroundings, may thus for many of us require a fundamental change in our ways of thinking (Davidson, 30, 80).

In the case being examined here, it is a matter of faith's being considered as part of a particular kind of general system, namely a general *religious* system. Within such a system there may be elements that in themselves constitute smaller systems; these are called subsystems (Miller, 30–31, 52–55, 665–66), an example of which would be the system of governance that is part of a religion's social structure.

Synthesizing Systems—Making Sense of Settings

Another important collection of elements constitutes a separate category in a religious system. Such collections are what in system theory can be called synthesizing systems. Their position in the religious system is shown in figure B. Here, the relationship of faith to the other elements in the system is more precisely illustrated. The influence of these elements on faith is in fact indirect. This is shown by the convergence of arrows from them onto the synthesizing systems and by the ascent of an arrow from the synthesizing systems to faith. Faith's more direct influence on the other elements is shown by the arrow from faith to feelings.

Figure B. A General Religious System with Its Synthesizing Systems

The influence of the system on faith is not haphazard. Because of their synthesizing systems, believers sense that the other elements of the system coalesce in a meaningful way. A synthesizing system is thus a personal or shared disposition by which a general system is personally or commonly accepted. Such a disposition is a more delineated component of a less specified "cognitive system," namely, the general awareness and feeling by which a person interacts coherently with a larger environment (Laszlo, 120, 127, 239).

A synthesizing system may be a simple, nearly intuitive disposition (like a religious feeling), a highly refined and conceptual framework (like a theology), or any combinations of these with any other individuating characteristics. Whatever the case, for religious systems it is an interpretive pattern that serves as a kind of internal clearinghouse for the large collection of elements with which religiousness is involved. This coalescence of the elements of the general religious system, *as sensed, appreciated, and/or understood by the devotee,* constitutes a personal system by which the devotee interprets religion and life and is able to live in a relatively satisfying way. As an interpretive system, it functions like many other systems that help take a variety of impressions or a variety of elements of a general system and put them into an "orderly package" by which an individual can live or operate within general or other systems.

Some examples of countless other synthesizing systems that facilitate understanding and communication are philosophy, political science, and management theory (Dillon, 11–13). These are formal and elaborate synthesizing systems; but as in general religious systems, simpler systems based on common sense or insights born of experience may also serve a synthesizing role in various other general systems. In Christianity, for example, a synthesizing system would be whatever awareness, simple or complex, enables a given believer to feel that his or her Christian religion is meaningful.

It should be particularly noted that the elements of a synthesizing system include the elements of the general system but as internally appropriated. A synthesizing system may include other elements not in the general system of which it is a part but useful for an individual who is sharing the general system with others. Unique images or thought patterns would be such uncommon elements; for example, in a general religious system such as Christianity, a given Christian may imaginatively associate Jesus Christ—as the center of the Church—with a mainframe rather than more traditionally with a vine (John 15:5) or head (Ephesians 4:15–16). This is not to say, however, that the uncommon elements of a synthesizing system cannot eventually become common coin, that is, part of the general system. This may be what happened in times recounted in Hebrew Scripture when Yahweh came to be thought of by some as a loving spouse and not merely a just and protective overlord.

The complexity of synthesizing systems in a religion can range from the simple synthesizing system of the average believer to the complex and quite intellectualized synthesizing systems of theologians. Whatever the case, it is worth noting that the relationship of a general system and its synthesizing systems is one of mutual influence. Figure B shows this by the opposite directions of the arrow between faith and synthesizing systems. The general system significantly determines the nature of the synthesizing systems; and the synthesizing systems, through those who have adopted them, support and/or alter the general system. Simply put in religious terms, how believers think and feel about their religion is both influenced by and influences that religion. Christians' attitudes toward ministry, for example, are influenced by established patterns of the Christian religious system and in turn have an impact on the development of such patterns in that system. Thus individual Christians through their faith or theology can influence how other Christians believe.

Since a general system, including its synthesizing systems, may be one by which persons find meaning in life, it may also be called a meaning system. As specifically religious, a meaning system serves as a context in which persons acquire the basic resources for a satisfying existence, namely, the means of giving definition and direction to their lives (Bowker, 363, 372). For a believer, such a meaning system may also be paradigmatic in the sense that it becomes a governing model or meaningful instance of the way religiousness is possible. Practicing Jews, for example, may best understand religiousness in general or religiousness in another specific form (for example, Islam) by drawing on their experience as Jews; Judaism may be the experiential base of comparison. The coalescence of religious elements and subsystems into a general religious system is specific to individual religions; it is what distinguishes one religion from another, say Christianity from Hinduism. Believers often observe this in light of the paradigmatic nature of their respective religious systems.

Differentiated Systems—Related Settings

They also typically observe that there are multiple variations of the particular religious system that is the context of their faith. Thus systems also work to differentiate religiousness further, for example, from particular world religions into major groupings, denominations, local religious communities, and even into individual faith. For example, Christianity is divided into Roman Catholicism, Eastern Orthodoxy, and Protestantism. Each of these three major branches is further divided. Protestantism is divided into Lutheranism, Presbyterianism, and hundreds of other denominations. These denominations, like the denominations, or rites, of the other two major branches, are divided geographically and culturally into local congregations or parishes. Finally, not every member of a local religious community believes and practices in exactly the same way. Each may be religious according to an individualized variant of a larger shared system. One devotee may be more traditional, another more progressive; one may prefer certain prayers or customs, another others.

The general system, in this case Christianity, varies somewhat as certain features of the religion become associated with this or that group or individual. In other words, the general Christian system is divided into a large variety of differentiated systems that resemble one another by reason of certain elements and that are distinct from one another by reason of other elements. Thus the meaning systems of Eastern Orthodox and Protestant Christianity exclude submission to papal authority. Lutheran and Presbyterian forms of Protestant religiousness are characterized by differing theological traditions and by differing styles of worship. Within denominations, some congregations are more liberal and others more conservative. The same is true of individual believers within local groupings. These are but a few examples of the multiple kinds of differences that bring an immense variety to the differentiated systems through which the religiousness of a specific religion is lived out.

Such differences can include any of the religious system's elements or subsystems. Typically, the variety of synthesizing systems is a crucial factor in the subdivision of a religion. This is because of the central role of the synthesizing systems in inspiring loyalty to specific theologies, customs, institutions, and other parts of religious traditions. This loyalty, as part of what in literary theory is called a "web" in which texts are interpreted, often goes unnoticed (Boone, 2–3, 14, 18).

Within a particular religion there are—strictly speaking—as many synthesizing systems as there are believers. These systems are similar enough, however, for the believers to regard themselves as part of one congregation, denomination or rite, major branch, and/or religion or general religious system.

The Flexibility of Systems

The variability of systems within a given category points to the fact that systems, even religious ones, can be flexible, that certain elements can be changed without negating the essential characteristics of the given system. Here it is a matter of what in system theory is called an open system. In a closed system, all the elements are fixed so that the system invariably attains the goal, as does, say, a simple electrical system that energizes a house. In an open system, however, some elements are in flux to meet varying circumstances, and the normal purpose of the system may be attained with some diversification (Johnson, 146).

For example, as was observed earlier in this chapter, fundamentalist interpreters can vary or adapt their biblical interpretations to include some figurative meanings and still be regarded as fundamentalist. Such adaptability is possible for any activities or elements of a system. Awareness of this is important for both proponents and opponents of given systems. Otherwise, one, the other, or both might be inclined to identify *all* elements of one or the other system as intrinsic to it, though such identification may be unwarranted. This can lead to wholesale, unsubtle acceptance or disapproval. In light of the prevailing fundamentalist biblical interpretations, and because of the assumptions and institutions typically associated with a fundamentalist outlook, some people might be inclined to regard the fundamentalist approach as *intrinsically* patriarchal and sexist when such may not be the case. Whatever sexist elements exist in groups inclined toward fundamentalist interpretation need not be permanent features even if at one point they are deemed permanently desirable. Granted, changing such features will likely affect the whole system, including the synthesizing systems within it, but these features can be changed without altering the elements that define the original system. Therefore, to reject any system for having a perceived or actual trait one rejects, is to run the risk of throwing the baby out with the bathwater. Examples of this would be rejecting fundamentalist interpretation for supposed irrationality or rejecting critical interpretation for supposed rationalism.

Religious Systems As Relative and Absolute

Various Paths to a Common Goal

Religious systems are multiple—or better, innumerable. They are the countless ways by which the divine or absolute is mediated to people. A mediation of the divine may be understood, then, as a means by which the divine is known to faith, a circumstance by which the divine comes to or is known by a believer. If all religious systems were regarded as fully or completely authentic—that is, as providing equivalent mediations of the divine—they would all be regarded as relative as well as equal. This means that while their characteristics might be perceived as different, they would all be thought to provide equivalent mediations of absolute meaning: one mediation, no matter what its singular characteristics, would be thought to be as good as another. The perceived equality could exemplify what in system theory has been called the principle of *equifinality* whereby the same end may be attained in varying ways and from differing initial circumstances because of the variability of open systems (Bertalanffy, 40). The disposition that gives rise to a sense of equal mediations of the divine is typical of Eastern religions. A devotee of Zen Buddhism or Raja Yoga may, for example, learn that there are many gods, many redeemers, or many religious customs but that all of these lead to the same end, total enlightenment or fully satisfying unity with what some call the divine.

Among Western religions, the admission that there are many relative and equal systems is quite evident in the acceptance of personal styles of faith within a local religious community and in the mutual recognition of denominations or rites within the larger branches of the religions. Individual members of local religious congregations are accepted as such so long as their systems of religiousness are congruent with the system that characterizes the community as a whole. In, say, a Catholic parish, it may make no difference to anyone whether some members prefer more devotions to Mary while others prefer more social action as long as all adhere to what they agree makes their style of Christianity basically Catholic. The same is true of denominations or rites: the differences between them are not so significant that the system of the larger branch of their religion cannot accommodate them. All of these cases provide examples of differentiated religious systems within a general religious system. They are variants of Christianity within the general Christian system.

Our Way Is Best

Religious systems are regarded as inauthentic (providing no mediation of the divine) or not fully authentic (providing a less than totally satisfactory mediation of the divine) to the extent that they do not seem to resemble or cannot be equated with a system regarded as normative. In other words, where devotees regard their religious system as the only true one or as the best one, other systems are regarded as no good or as less than best. This process may be called the absolutizing of one's religious system. Such absolutizing can from one perspective be understood as simply a form of oversimplification due to "information overload" or the difficulty of dealing with the complexity of the issues involved (see Miller, 147–50, 871). From another perspective, however, it can be perceived that in this situation the absoluteness of the divine or the meaningfulness that is mediated may be thought, rightly or wrongly, to be necessarily identified with the believer's mediating system, which in fact may be quite variable or at least a bit more variable than the believer assumes.

This means that a given system's mediation of the absolute may be taken as a sign that the system itself is absolute, that it is perfect as it is, permanent and essentially unchangeable (Jung, *Memories,* 154). When one takes a meaning system or system of interpretation to contain the entire meaning experienced, one can be said to comprehend meaning in a certain logical or definable sense within a certain frame of reference in which one draws conclusions allowed in this context. But one can also be said in such a case to be possibly losing an awareness of a greater meaning, namely, an indefinable larger context or power by which the understood meaning occurs (namely, from which it has arisen and toward which it is proceeding) (Johnson, 32–34). A sense of meaning from this perspective is just one experience on the way to a larger meaning. An as yet uncomprehended—or perhaps incomprehensible—horizon thus relativizes or renders transitory the meaning system in which one has found satisfaction.

From religious perspectives, this larger, elusive context can be associated with God as the source and end of all, including understood or perceived meanings. To confuse a meaningful experience of or statement about God with the very Godhead is at once to understand something about God (that God is meaningful) and to misunderstand what God is *all* about. That, it seems, is another reason why Augustine said that if you understand God, you do not understand. When devotees assume that they are relating to the divine through the mediation of an absolute system, they are often implying that their system, as essentially the only one up to the task, must retain *all* of its distinctive features to remain fully authentic.

Though frequently quite controversial, such a position may well be justified, at least in theory. For to deny the possibility could be to absolutize a meaning system by which the denial is claimed to be appropriate. In other words, someone who opposes absolutizing meaning systems can be equally absolutist in doing so; and this is self-contradictory. But the issues involved in deciding the extent to which a given religious system may or should be regarded as absolute can be quite complex. These will be discussed in chapter 3. Precedents for such an attitude vis-à-vis other religions can be seen in the claim of Hebrew Scripture or the Old Testament that the deities of the Gentile religions are no-gods (2 Chronicles 13:9; Jeremiah 2:11) and in the claim of Christian Scripture that there is no other name by which to be saved than that of Jesus Christ (Acts 4:12). The legitimacy of these claims is not for the moment under discussion, although admittedly many believers make such claims. Suffice it to say that in both Scriptures there can be found— or at least perceived—counterclaims that give a less apodictic or more dialectic, multisided picture of biblical teachings on other religions (for example, Genesis 9:17; Malachi 1:11; Matthew 22:40; Mark 7:28). The issue is, therefore, in the view of many, not quickly settled. What is to be observed here is a precedent for absolutizing a given religious system.

There Is No God but Ours

An inclination to absolutize in such a manner is thus under-standable in light of the religious system's nature. Since it is a mediation of the absolute or God, it can, even if relative or variable, be taken to be as absolute as what it mediates. Godly qualities appreciable in the absolute are thus attributed to the religious system itself. God as so perceived then becomes for the perceiver the God who cannot be fully perceived, or perceived at all, in any other way. For example, one can say that one's religion is a mediation of the truly divine; and from there one can move to a claim that this religion must be, if not the only true mediation of the divine, at least the truest. Since such an inference is common in the West, it seems right to say that the absolutizing of religious systems is an overt tendency among Westerners. This observation need not, however, be taken as an assertion that similar inferences are unknown in the East.

Absolutizing a Fundamentalist or Critical System

We Are Right, and You Are Wrong

This absolutizing tendency can be seen as a major factor in the disharmony between fundamentalist and critical interpreters. These discordant systems of biblical interpretation constitute subsystems within larger Christian differentiated systems. Both subsystems typically include believers who claim a high degree of objective truth. While both are influenced by the Western religious tendency to absolutize, critical interpreters may be further and directly influenced by the prizing of objectivity through various sorts of academic study or scientific investigation. Members of each of the two groups interpreting the Bible may regard the other subsystem as inauthentic or not totally authentic. The fundamentalist interpreters may regard the critical interpreters as totally or partially heretical; the critical interpreters may regard their fundamentalist counterparts as benighted or somewhat unenlightened. Each group, in accord with principles it holds to be the most meaningful, and in the context of all the elements of its differentiated religious system, has found an approach to the Bible and to biblical truth that—as it is assumed or even demonstrated within each system—accords with truth itself or the truth of the divine. The two appear as opposing cultures. In either case, the judgment regarding the other can be seen to be made in accord with the absolutizing of a system, namely, of a subsystem (biblical interpretation) within the general Christian system and its differentiated systems.

Or How Wrong Are You?

The legitimacy of one claim or the other depends in great measure on the nature of Christianity as a system of religiousness. Does the overriding system that characterizes Christianity as a specific religion necessarily need to exclude, totally or in part, either the fundamentalist or the critical approach to the Bible? The question is about the essential characteristics of these two systems. This is the question to be discussed in subsequent chapters. Any approach to such a question must apparently be taken in the context of a given system. It is hoped that the general Christian religious system presupposed and partially expounded in the next chapter is acceptable enough to a sufficiently large number of Christians that in the rest of this book the fuller discussion of the suggested issues will find a hearing among all who are parties to exegetical rivalry.

Summary

The critical interpretation of the Bible represents a preference for assumptions and methodologies that allow readers or hearers of the sacred text to move considerably beyond literal understanding. The fundamentalist approach is more restrictive, displaying a marked preference for literalness in the interpretation of scriptural stories and norms. Proponents of these alternate approaches to the Bible often oppose one another vehemently. When it takes the form of exegetical rivalry between believing Christians, this vehemence appears to be rooted in each group's absolutizing of its specific religious system. It is the nature of faith to provide a sense of absolute meaning, and there is precedent in the Christian tradition to absolutize the general Christian system. It is, therefore, understandable how such absolutizing, for better or for worse, can be carried over into specific or differentiated religious systems that include views on the interpretation of the Bible. Viewed in this way, Christianity is characterized by two cultures of belief. The extent to which this is justified appears to depend on the nature of Christianity, or at least on its nature as perceived within a given system such as the one propounded in this book.

Chapter 2

Christianity
<u>As a System</u>

Main Elements of the System

D espite the multiplicity of differentiated systems that are characteristic of Christianity in all its subdivisions, it seems possible to say that there is an overriding or general system, one that most Christians share and that allows Christianity to be identifiable as a single and distinctive religion. Elements of this general system that are prominent include Jesus Christ, his Cross, his Resurrection, the Church, and the Bible.

As is typical of components of a meaning system, the elements are varied and might be categorized under more than one heading, including historical personalities, historical events, communities, literary works, concepts, doctrines, or theologies. They thus relate to the feelings, activities, objects, social structures, images

27

and concepts, and synthesizing systems of religious systems, though not falling into neat categories. Jesus Christ is, according to most Christians' religious systems, a historical personality whose enormous impact on the world and on Christians has been assessed in terms of multiple concepts, doctrines, and theologies. Such elements are typically rooted in Scripture and elaborated in later teaching. Access to him as a personality can thus be indirect, mediated through other elements. Likewise, the Cross and Resurrection are commonly accepted as major events and also as two of the most important concepts influencing interpretations of Jesus Christ's significance. The Church is a social grouping or community of persons believing in Jesus Christ as Redeemer. And the Bible is a literary work of a special kind, being for Christians a primary source of the concepts, doctrines, and theologies that influence the understanding of the entire Christian religious system.

Thus these elements are, along with others such as the Eucharistic ritual or the doctrine of the Trinity, part of the total content and context of the faith by which Christians live and find meaning. Such elements constitute a general religious system and can be explained one by one as typically perceived by Christians within their particular religious system.

Jesus Christ

Jesus Christ is the focal point of the system. He is the one through whom God communicates love to the Christian (1 John 3:16). This love needs to be accepted in faith, for through this love and faith the Christian is saved. That is to say that through this acceptance, the Christian enters into a satisfying relationship with God, a relationship that allows the Christian to experience absolute meaning. Because the reliability of this love appears as permanent, the Christian's acceptance is also characterized by firm and assuring hope (Romans 15:13). This Jesus Christ is not merely the memory of a personality from the past. According to the faith he stimulates and nurtures, he is a living personality; he lives now, albeit in a way that is at present deemed extraordinary. His present existence is regarded as "glorified," which is to say full of the perfecting power of God.

Jesus Christ has risen from the dead; he is now no longer susceptible to human tragedy nor limited to time and space as humans usually are. His body radiates with God's renewing grace; he lives forever (1 Corinthians 15:40–42). He is usually not experienced empirically or through the ordinary senses, though there have been claims of such encounters in both New Testament times and later ages. Rather, Christians most often meet him through the other elements of the Christian system, most typically through the devoted use of or involvement with the Bible, the Christian community, personal prayer, and the sacraments or other rituals. He can even be met in the world among other persons—notably in the poor—or in the wonders of nature.

The extent to which the world belongs to the Christian system will be more precisely delineated below. Here it is sufficient to observe that through this system faith knows the presence of this risen and loving Jesus Christ.

His character and personality traits too are made apparent to faith through the elements of the system. Thus in prayer or in a moment of interaction with another person, the believing Christian may be struck by Jesus' compassion. A most important means of contact with the qualities of Jesus Christ is the Bible. Here are to be found many stories about his life and teachings. These stories are mostly set in the time before his death. They exhibit qualities and powers, however, that the risen Jesus still possesses. So he can still be turned to for, say, forgiveness or healing. The stories also constitute a reliable source of his message. So they say to the Christian that Jesus Christ continues to communicate words that challenge, console, encourage, or praise.

Such words have for the Christian a particular power and value because they are believed to be associated with divinity itself. To most Christians, this means more than that Jesus Christ is, like the prophets, a mouthpiece of God. It means that Jesus Christ enjoys an identity with God that is unique among human beings. He is called "the Son of God." His sonship is not merely like the status that the ancient kings of Israel were said to enjoy, and not merely like that dignity by which all believers are called children of God. The sonship of Jesus Christ identifies him as the one who, though truly human, is also endowed with the nature of the very Godhead.

This conviction regarding Jesus' identity is believed to be clearly communicated in the Bible. For some Christians, this communication is understood to occur mostly by inference, that is, by the use of titles that can refer to God but that even in the Bible do not always do so necessarily. Such titles or terms include *Son of God, Savior,* and *Lord.* Their meaning is made less ambiguous respecting Jesus Christ's divinity by a few direct scriptural assertions that he is God (for example, John 1:1 and 20:28; Hebrews 1:7–8) and quite significantly by Church traditions holding that Jesus Christ is unambiguously truly God. Typical witnesses of these traditions are the teachings of the Councils of Nicaea and Chalcedon from the fourth and fifth centuries.

The Cross

The passion stories or the other New Testament passages regarding Jesus' death are particularly valuable for putting the believer in contact with another major element of the Christian system, the Cross. This, of course, still relates to Jesus' identity and significance for the Christian. What the Cross particularly highlights, though, is the importance of Jesus Christ as the Redeemer. This risen Jesus Christ who bears the wounds in his body is one who has offered his entire self on behalf of others. The Bible depicts his suffering and death as acts of obedience that in a mysterious but effective way atone for the sins of humanity (for example, Matthew 26:28), the sins that have been the source of grief and tragedy in this present world.

This does not mean that grief and tragedy have been eliminated from the world. Rather, it asserts that the sordid energy of the faults and evil that would permanently mar God's cosmic work—a creation God originally saw as "very good" (Genesis 1:31)—has been cut off at its source. This energy retains its vicious influence. Yet the day will come when the risen Jesus Christ will appear in splendor to judge all humanity and when those who have lived righteously will enter a heavenly state in which grief and tragedy have no more place. The Cross, then, is an essential ingredient of the Christians' sense of ultimate meaning. Because of the Cross, they can sense in faith that the faults, grief, and tragedy that plague their world are ultimately powerless over it (1 Corinthians 1:18). They can sense forgiveness of their sins and live in lively hope of perfect happiness. And all of this is so because of God's loving plan and historical gesture.

God has not left believers lost in the present world but has lovingly intervened to save them from sin, suffering, and death. Jesus' passion is thus a revelation of God's compassion for a sorrowing people. The Bible does not completely explain the reasons for such sorrow, especially for the apparently disproportionate distribution of it among those who seem less deserving of it. Yet the Bible makes it clear that God does not remain aloof from the pitiable aspects of the worldly scene but through Jesus Christ, God's Son, enters into them, is afflicted by them, and thus reorients God's wounded creation toward eventual heavenly glory.

The Resurrection

The redemptive and reorienting power of the Cross works in tandem with the Resurrection. Jesus Christ's rising from the dead is thus another major element of the Christian system. If through the Cross God reveals a compassionate will to participate in the grief-ridden human scene, through the Resurrection God reveals a merciful design to renew a people suffering from sin. By rising, Jesus Christ becomes the one through whom human sin, suffering, and death lead to a wonderful transformation. Here, God reveals that these afflictions are by God's power ultimately insignificant. The world's tragedies are moments of trial and transition that can now lead not to condemnation and continued torment but to vindication and joy (1 Peter 1:8). This reversal is thorough and complete, for Jesus Christ now reigns with the Father, enjoying with him all the glory that is God's.

This is a glory that belongs to Christ not only as the "Son of God" in the special sense connoting divinity but also as the Son who is truly human. His glory, then, is not only that which was his before he was born in the human condition but that which radiates from and through his transformed, risen human body (John 1:14). In Jesus Christ, humanity itself is glorified. Without the Resurrection, the Cross remains powerless (1 Corinthians 15:17). Without the Cross, the Resurrection might be little more than a miraculous resuscitation (1 Corinthians 15:3).

The Church

The mutual influence of Cross and Resurrection makes them mutually dependent and thus inseparable to Christians as redemptive acts. Another element of the Christian system, the Church, enjoys a similar inseparability from the Cross and Resurrection. The Christian Scripture, especially the Pauline literature, depicts the crucified and risen Jesus Christ's exaltation as a cosmic event. This means that his transition from death to life has radically influenced all of creation. For the Son who dwelled with God the Father before creation was the very agent by whom God called all finite realities into existence and by whom God continues to keep them in harmony. So, following the influence of Greek philosophical systems, the Son is also given the titles *Word* and *First-born*.

By this same power, by this same Son or Word, God entered the created scene, becoming one with it by identity with Jesus Christ. Once this Christ is risen, once he emerges from creation made tragic and pitiful by sin, the cosmos relates to God in a new way (Colossians 1:19–20). The intimacy of the created with the creator is intensified. Thus all of the created order, by association with Jesus Christ as both the divine creative power and as a fellow-creature of finite nature, is made ready for intimacy with God in a new way. It is the way in which sin, suffering, and death lose out to holiness, joy, and immortality.

This readiness, which already constitutes a radical transformation of the universe, becomes an actual and explicit intimacy in those who associate themselves with Jesus Christ. This association, initiated by faith in him and sacramentally or ritually enacted through the rite of baptism (Romans 6:3–4), constitutes membership in the ecclesial or Church community. The Church, then, is believed to be the body of believers who, commonly living within the Christian system, participate in the new intimacy with

God that was established through Jesus Christ's death and Resurrection. They see themselves as in fact participating in that very death and Resurrection and thus profiting from the redemptive character of Jesus Christ's exaltation. They are thus constrained to participate, through loving service of those in need, in Jesus Christ's compassionate alleviation of the world's tragic suffering.

This participation is effected by grace, by the loving favor of God (Romans 3:24, 5:2) that comes as the Holy Spirit (Romans 5:51, 1 Corinthians 6:11). John the Evangelist's account of Jesus' breathing on the apostles after his Resurrection (John 20:22) proclaims that this Jesus Christ sent by God the Father to be glorified now sends the Spirit for the similar glorification of those who believe. As the Church, they assure that the glory of Jesus Christ's death and Resurrection does not redound to him alone but as well to those associated with him. Thus the redemptive character of his glorious intimacy with God the Father, as a visible actualization and not merely as a cosmic openness, is dependent on a Church transformed by God's grace, as though the life of faith, as living water, goes back from believers to Christ (John 4:7), the source of grace or living water. For the Church, as a community of the redeemed, depends on Jesus Christ's Cross and Resurrection (Ephesians 5:25–27). Thus the Church and the full redemptive act of God in Jesus Christ have, by the miracle and support of grace, become mutually dependent.

The Bible

A consideration of Jesus Christ, the Cross, the Resurrection, and the Church makes the intricacy of the Christian system quite apparent. For these four elements of belief are closely knit and mutually supportive. The full identity of Jesus Christ necessarily entails the effects of his suffering, death, and Resurrection. The full redemptive character of these events, in turn, necessarily entails the belief of the Church. This reveals how the life of the Church is essentially constituted as a continued relationship with Jesus Christ as Redeemer.

Since this relationship is expounded in the Bible, the importance of this fifth major element of the Christian system is eminently understandable. It is intimately associated with the other four through a mutual dependence similar to that which the first four enjoy with one another. For the Bible, by the power and inspiration of God, is both the product of believers and the work to which believers turn for inspiration and education. As both the Hebrew Scripture and the Christian New Testament, the Bible contains the inspired teachings, proclamations, prayers, reflections, meditations, and historical memories of those who through faith have been able to see God's loving and redeeming work in their lives. In this sense the Bible, and more specifically the Christian Bible, is in its writing, editing, and canonization dependent on the Church that experiences itself in faith as a people enjoying a redemptive association with the crucified and risen Jesus Christ.

By means of the canonization process, the Church, guided by the Holy Spirit, selects the literary works that belong in the Bible and acknowledges the Bible's high status and authority. For in it the other elements of the Christian system are defined, proclaimed, and explained. So the members of the Church that produced the Bible are dependent on the Bible for their very identity as Christians.

A System of Grace

No more than any other element of the Christian system is the Bible the product of merely human initiative. For the Bible results not merely from human historical and literary talent but more eminently from the inspiration of God. This perception of the Bible arises within the context of the general Christian system and is especially related to Jesus Christ's gift of the Spirit by which the believing Church is constituted. The divine inspiration of the Bible, then, is an effect of grace.

Something similar must be said of all the other elements of the system. Christians do not view Jesus Christ, his Cross and Resurrection, and the Church founded in him as constituting a meaning system that emerges merely from human creativity. While human initiative is part of the system-forming process, each of the elements is understood as first and foremost the result of God's initiative and grace. So the entire system is understood from within the system as one that is preeminently God's work, a work with which God lovingly endows the earth for the sake of salvation.

Summary

Jesus Christ, his Cross and Resurrection, the Church, and the Bible constitute the main elements of a religious system on which most Christians agree. These elements are so interrelated that, by the influence of divine grace, they are mutually dependent and supportive. As part of a general religious system, they allow the worldwide body of Christian believers to sense enough solidarity that Christianity can be distinguished from other religions of the world.

Chapter 3

Risks of Absolutizing

Denial of Absolutizing

This Is How It Is

The preceding chapter attempted to depict a basic religious system that is common to most Christians. It made no attempt to delineate differentiations of the system that come by way of varying theological traditions, of varying views of Church polity, or of any of the multiple other elaborations that, along with the fundamentalist and critical approaches to the Bible, make for the various subdivisions within Christianity. It was noted in chapter 1 that the last-named elaborations are often today decisive elements in the process of absolutizing the respective systems. Thus, certain styles of Christianity may be deemed to be the true or truest form of Christian faith or religiousness, whether the fundamentalist or critical approach to the Bible predominates. The same must be said of other elaborations. For example, one denomination, because of its particular origins or traditions, may call itself the truest; another, because of its particular form of governance, may claim ultimate authority in matters Christian; and so forth.

All such differentiated Christian systems are liable to include the element of absolutizing. A basic reason for this was suggested in chapter 1: the absolute thought to be mediated by the system can become so identified with the system that the absolute or divine is thought to be best appreciated only in this particular way, namely, through this particular system with all of its elements. It should be recalled that at the moment, the legitimacy of absolutizing Christianity itself or the general Christian system is not under discussion. This will be considered in chapter 6. Here, it is the matter of considering how differentiated Christian systems are absolutized and how such absolutizing might or might not be legitimate. What is typical of all of them is their tendency to deny that any absolutizing, as a purely subjective act, has taken place. This is clearly noticeable in both cultures of belief, namely in both fundamentalist Christian systems and critical Christian systems.

We Do Not Make It So

Absolutizing is, at least in part, a subjective act; that is, it is a personal response of an individual or group to an object of attention. Within religious systems, the respondents are the believers who declare that one of their objects of attention, in this case their system, is absolute. Thus, Roman Catholics may declare that theirs is the branch of the Church in which subsists the fullest expression of Christianity; fundamentalist interpreters may declare that denying the historicity of parts of the gospels is heresy; critically oriented Christians may declare that a certain conservative type of faith is narrow-minded dogmatism.

None of these believers, however, and no proponent of any other differentiated Christian system, is likely to want to declare that the absolutizing is *purely* his or her doing. Rather, the tendency is to want to declare that one is dealing with objective truths. The system is thus declared absolute because—so the claim goes— this is the way things are in themselves. Absolutizing happens because, according to this view, the objective facts or the verifiable conclusions compel it. For example, if the Roman Catholic hierarchy is absolutely declared the ultimate authority in Christian teaching and practice, it is because, according to this church's teaching and faith, that is the case by divine design. If the interpretation of the Bible in a fundamentalist way is the best for understanding the Christian system, it is because for fundamentalist interpreters that is what the very nature of the Bible requires by divine ordinance. If the critical approach to the Bible is the preferred one, that is because the evidence supporting this methodology appears to critical interpreters to accord with the truth as it is in itself or as God knows it.

Absolutizing in these instances may be understood as a subjective declaration, but not purely so. For the perceived facts make the system appear to each claimant as self-absolutizing in the sense that they call for the subjective recognition of their truth. Absolutizing is thus accorded a strong element of objectivity and is legitimized. Neither the fundamentalist nor the critical interpreters may want to claim that they have simply *declared* their method the better one. Rather, members of each group typically claim that their absolutizing is legitimate because their method is truly and objectively better.

It Is Quite Clear to Us

Once such a stance is taken, from one side or the other, it can become nearly impossible to refute. Believers who absolutize can allow themselves to become impervious to any other viewpoint. When this happens, they may have, by their subjective declarations or by the compelling nature of the objects considered, become locked into the system they perceive as absolute and may recognize no other as equal. From this position there may naturally appear no need to recognize the equality of another system; after all, this one appears in fact to be the best. A way to provoke such recognition would be to demonstrate the value of the alternate system. But that is precisely what is so repellent for many who are already firmly entrenched in their own. So the fundamentalist and the critical interpreter can remain unpersuaded regarding the value of the other's system. From the earliest years of fundamentalist interpretation, such entrenchment has been observable in the debates that separated this approach from its critics (Marsden, *Culture*, 215). But need this necessarily remain the case?

The Possible Rightness of Absolutizing

Surely It Could Be So

Being entrenched in a religious system is somewhat like being convinced that no one but one's beloved will do. No amount of argumentation can bring the starry-eyed lover to admit that there are "other fish in the sea." Surely, much is to be said for the lover's exclusive commitment; that is part of what makes the relationship so satisfying and meaningful. And one must apparently concede that it is quite possible—perhaps for reasons both on earth and in heaven—that there really is no other "fish." How, at any rate, could one prove the contrary to someone passionately fixed on his or her beloved? The same seems to be true of religious commitment within a given meaning system. By what vision could a mortal exclude from God's options a preference for such an arrangement? It would seem possible for the divine to be so intensely identified with one religious system, even with a single differentiation of a general religious system, that the divine's equal identification with all other such systems is excluded. The rightness of such absolutizing can then be regarded as a real possibility.

Surely It "Is" So

So, for example, one can say that theoretically the crucified and risen Jesus Christ can be known by the Church fully and most satisfactorily through either a fundamentalist or a critical interpretation of the Bible, but not through both. This would be the case if the absolutizing of one of these two elaborated Christian systems was in fact not purely subjective but a subjective response to what is objectively the case. Both sides would be claiming such. One side, however, would be deluded regarding its objectivity, while the other would not be.

Absolutizing as Faith

We Believe It Is So

A way to judge whether the objective facts support one's absolutizing is to use some criteria outside the system, namely other evidence or another interpretive system. But the absolutizing of a religious system as a claim to ultimate objective truth usually does not permit this. No other evidence or system of meaning is perceived to equal it. So the devotees may feel in their commitment that they have attained absolute objective truth even though they may have, by that same commitment, stopped short of such truth. At the point where they accept no more guarantees or measures of certitude, they trust and believe. It is like asserting that there really is no other "fish in the sea." Whatever objectivity there is remains a matter of faith because the perceived truth is entrenched in a love that does not look beyond its own sentiments and that influences judgments regarding the truth.

Faith or belief, as observed in chapter 1, is an acceptance of that by which one finds meaning, the assurance that one is right, or the surety that one is living and acting rightly. In the case of fundamentalist interpreters, this belief takes the form of accepting the general Christian system as differentiated through great faith and confidence in a mostly literal interpretation of the Bible. For those who approach the Bible critically, this belief takes the form of accepting the same general system but as differentiated through great faith and confidence in systems of critical analysis and methods of persuasive verification. Each group has claimants within its respective system that its faith is absolutely the best.

There Is No Getting Around Belief

But in either case the claimant is still subjectively absolutizing, even if the stance is not purely subjective; that is, even if it is a subjective response to what really is objectively so, it is still an act of faith. Even if there really are no other "fish in the sea," the awareness of this is based on the subjective disposition toward "other fish," not merely on the objective unsuitability of the "other fish" for the subject. And that is because the claimant assumes that he or she has the most reliable evidence or is making the judgment from within the most reliable meaning system. So the claimant's way of knowing is solely, or at least quite markedly, an act of believing. As an act of believing, it is a personal openness that expresses confidence in the systemic elements influencing it in its response to its object of attention. Such faith is perceptible even in the simple act of believing in the existence of common objects of everyday experience. For example, I believe—I trust my experience—that I am sitting in a chair; not to so believe seems idiotic, at least to a person of sound mind. My trust is so firm and healthy that I even say I *know* that I am sitting in a chair.

In the case of Christian faith, the ultimate object of such attention is God, the Father of the Lord Jesus Christ, who is known as mediated through the entire Christian system. But it has been argued persuasively that this kind of confidence connected with an object of attention is typical of any meaningful claim within any system, religious or otherwise (Wittgenstein, especially 12–21, 32, 72–75). It would, then, even be typical of a claim that would deny the theoretical possibility of the divine's full identification with any single religious system or with multiple systems. Here too the claimant would be making an assertion under the compelling influence of the system by which she or he is ultimately being guided. This is a subjective act that ultimately must be *believed* to be in accord with objective facts. From this perspective, there is a way to claim something is true within a given system but no way to know it is true without faith. The requisite faith need not necessarily be religious but must at least be a confidence that relinquishes totally objective absolute certainty, namely, an uncompromising conviction that one "knows" something without any faith whatever. A claim to truth would then accept meaningfulness and certainty within some belief system or meaning system. From this perspective, even theological or biblical declarations that, from their perspectives, rightly claim that God can be known about without a particular religious belief (for example, Romans 1:19) appear to be referring to a type of knowledge that involves belief of some kind.

Thus, an observation that knowledge of truth is ultimately contextual and inextricably tied to faith need not lead to a so-called deconstructionist denial of such knowledge or the truth of statements about it. It can surely lead to caution about presumptions regarding the knowledge of truth. But the confidence of belief within a system may be a viable, albeit fallible, way of holding to the truth to the extent to which it can be known (Tracy, 59–61, 87–88). Even deconstructionism, in its essential designs as a philosophical argument, is occupied with elucidating the elements by which statements both enjoy their power and bear their weaknesses (Johnson, 66–67).

You Could Be Right

Within the meaning system assumed for the writing of these reflections, it seems best to say that theoretically the divine can fully identify with a single elaborated religious system or with more than one such system. It is like saying that there may be only one fish in the sea or there may be more, but I do not assume that I am able to know which is true with total objectivity. A Christian's claim to such objectivity may be named the fallacy of Christian certitude. This amounts to saying that in their confident and receptive awareness within the Christian belief system, theoretically *either* the fundamentalist *or* the critical interpreters of the Bible could be right in their claim to full authenticity. Such an admission may involve an unnerving risk of one's present certainty (Tracy, 93, 98–99). But the admission also means that theoretically *both* could be right and in equally respectable ways.

This makes sense if one accepts the possibility that differing and even apparently contradictory perspectives on ultimate truth can in a certain way complement one another. The acceptance of such a possibility has been the basis of numerous concepts, such as Nicholas of Cusa's coincidence of opposites or Einstein's relativity (Bertalanffy, 239–48). For both fundamentalist and critical interpreters eyeing one another's systems, this kind of acceptance may be a very hard pill to swallow, especially if one of them identifies with the essence of the other's system any variable traits that are perceived as undesirable, for example, if the fundamentalist approach is judged as essentially sexist or the critical approach is judged as essentially rationalist.

But granting claims regarding biblical interpretation seems, within the general Christian system proposed in chapter 2, to be quite appropriate in view of the success of each of these interpretive systems at being, for different believers, an important element in recognizing the God of Jesus Christ. From this perspective, it seems profitable to reflect on the respective advantages of each system and to speculate on what the implications might be if one or the other of these cultures is objectively absolute, supreme, or fully authentic.

Assets of Fundamentalist Interpretation

Direct and Clear

There is an admirable clarity to the fundamentalist view. It is clean, polished, and without complicating encumbrances. Since the biblical stories and moral directives are by and large accepted at face value, the believer can enjoy them unquestioningly and freely relish their colors, imagery, or luminosity. In a world of confused or conflicting values, one can submit to expressions of divine authority clearly perceived (Neuhaus, 17–18). The impact of the biblical message is thus immediate and delighting (Branick, 24) and is not detoured through multiple conscious interpretive filters. The creation story or the stories about Jesus, for example, are simply taken as they stand. This unguardedness, innocent of the often ponderous dispositions of more complex interpretations of the Bible, may be closely related to the childlike attitude that

Jesus said was indispensable for entry into the kingdom of heaven (for example, Mark 10:15).

Uncompromisingly Religious

Such innocence allows the fundamentalist approach to be unambiguous regarding the transcendent and supernatural character of the divine (Noll, 143–44). This is a valuable feature in a general Christian system perceived as a system of grace. In contrast, where there is ambiguity on this point—say, in theologies that emphasize divine immanence, or in metaphysical systems influenced by scientific positivism, or, at the other extreme, monism—the impression can be given that the divine either does not really exist, is irrelevant to the human enterprise, or is identical with the human enterprise. In its origins, the fundamentalist approach was not so much adverse to modern sciences as to what it considered inauthentic science that *a priori* excluded the possibility of the supernatural and miraculous (Marsden, *Culture,* 120–21, 214). The fundamentalist approach seeks to harmonize—namely, to bring into a mutually beneficial alignment—traditional religious wisdom and what fundamentalist interpreters perceive as the most admirable features of modern science (Mendelsohn, 23–24). In sum, fundamentalist interpreters cannot easily be accused of endangering the full realization of cherished Christian aspirations by denying the real and redeeming impact of God (Ashcraft, 537) on a humanity that can accept God's existence and welcome God's powerful influence.

Here, fundamentalist interpreters remain a strong bulwark against a narrow secularism that is repugnant to Christianity generally. And by their readiness to accept the facticity of such astounding biblical phenomena as faith healings, visions, prophecy, or miracles, they are already aligned with branches of study in which such paranormal phenomena as clairvoyance and psychokinesis are rapidly gaining respectability. Advancement like this is being made under the influence of such disciplines as holistic medicine, transpersonal psychology, and Jungian psychology. In this regard, the fundamentalist approach overlaps at least in part the charismatic movement within Christianity, although many fundamentalist interpreters do not admit the duration of paranormal phenomena beyond biblical times (Falwell, Dobson, and Hindson, 133–38).

Understandably, then, fundamentalist interpreters are said to be characteristically reactionary with respect to modernity (Nielsen, viii, 3, 23, 148), especially such forms of it that, since the eighteenth century, have been opposed to strong and privileged religious authority (Marty and Appleby, *Glory*, 11–12, 26, 176). This claim seems to hold with respect to the secularist leanings of much that is modern. Yet with respect to interest in the paranormal, the fundamentalist approach may be finding itself aligned with the most modern thinking and research. Such an alignment is even more discernible as science itself, along with and assisted by philosophy, feminist studies, and other scholarly pursuits, seriously questions whether many of its established assumptions are too narrow (Mendelsohn, 34).

More Than a Head Trip

Moreover, within the fundamentalist system, the biblical stories especially communicate to what many scholars today designate as the "right brain." Fundamentalist interpreters themselves often speak of "heart knowledge" that is opposed to "head knowledge" (Ammerman, 73, 131). These designations seem more or less to conform to a differentiation between the "right" and "left" brains. Because each hemisphere of the brain appears to be distinguishable by functions that are dominant but not necessarily exclusive to it, the distinction according to "right" and "left" may not be totally proper (Springer and Deutsch, 29–63, 277–79, 282–83).

It does seem clear that the entire brain is associated with the complete range of cognitive functions. Nonetheless, *right* is popularly used to name that part or function of the brain on which persons rely in responding to reality intuitively, emotionally, and holistically. *Left* is used to name that part or function associated with analyzing, categorizing, and making deductions (Springer and Deutsch, 272–275). The right side complements the left by responding to objects in their totality; the impression on the right side is characterized by an unreflecting and intuitive sense of the unity and significance of all the object's components; here, images and feelings, rather than concepts and distinctions, determine knowing or response.

So, for example, one can watch a sunrise and respond to it or understand it in various ways. With the left side of one's brain predominately active, one can reflect on the state of the gases that compose the fiery star, note the astronomical conditions that allow a certain planet or the moon still to be somewhat visible, observe the meteorological conditions that account for the celestial hues and cloud formations, or comment on the pollutants that influence the sun's apparent color. With the right side of one's brain predominately active, one can marvel at the splendorous array of colors, gasp at the power of this mighty star, be thankful for its warmth, find hope in a newborn day, or sense something of the dawn of life itself in the mystery of creation.

Likewise, one can respond to biblical stories in various ways. Jesus' post-Resurrection appearances can serve as an example. A believer can respond to them rather conceptually by recalling that Jesus Christ's victory over death is essential to a Christian's sense of meaning, by speculating on the nature of Christ's relationship to matter and space at this point, by attempting to establish the psychological state of those who witnessed him, or by commenting on the degree to which history is part of the literary form whereby the appearances are depicted. Or in a more emotional way, one can marvel at the power of God who has wrought such a transformation, be comforted by the words of this loving Redeemer, feel reborn in one's own life, feel optimistic about what joy awaits beyond the grave, or sense something of the compassion of a divine, loving God. In the latter responses, the activity of the right brain predominates, allowing for a certain exuberance and élan that is frequently idle in a highly left-brain response. And the direct and spontaneous fundamentalist interpretation of the biblical texts facilitates the right-brain predominance.

Reassuring

If objective facts justify absolutizing this interpretation, then it is as if God is inviting the believing Christian to approach the divine presence unquestioningly and with utter trust in the mostly literal truth of God's biblical word. God's self, message, and will are being directly and unambiguously communicated: this loving act requires only the believer's open acceptance and the heartfelt joy of life in God's grace. Here there is much security. The fundamentalist approach, then, can provide a great deal of comfort and bring its adherents much confidence (Ammerman, 191). They can rest assured that they know, to the letter, God's will, even if it requires suffering (Ammerman, 41–48, 66, 188). In such security, Christians walk with God in the simple trust of children holding the hands of their parents or elders.

Assets of Critical Interpretation

Intellectually Compelling

There is a certain refinement to the critical interpretation of the Bible. Sensitivity to the background, composition, and aims of the texts appeals to many in an age when the various academic disciplines have done so much to account for the intricate and often mysterious workings of the physical world, the human psyche, and the social order. The findings of the various sciences are vast and serve as an awesome monument to human intelligence and to the wisdom of God, in whose image, by biblical teaching, humanity is made (Genesis 1:27). It seems imperative then to bring this intelligence to bear no less on the Bible than on anything else.

Not that scholarly knowledge becomes necessarily a substitute for faith. Rather, such knowledge can complement the faith of someone whose mind and heart seem to need a religious awareness that uncritical approaches to the Bible do not help actuate. Here, it is the case of believers' desiring in this scientific age a strong intellectual element of a specific analytical kind in their religious system. As Christians, they want to include in their system—along with the five main elements discussed in the last chapter—certain conclusions of the scholarly order. In their view, this brings them an enhanced sense of satisfaction in their religion (McKnight, 44) and thus a satisfying sense of closeness to God or of rightness with God.

Modern in Mentality

Their particular sensitivity to the workings of the created and human order can help evoke in them particular views of how God intervenes in this order. Such views often have limited room for the sudden, the dramatic, the astounding, the sensational, or anything that appears to violate natural or ordinary processes as perceived through human intelligence under the influence of the modern sciences. This is not meant to diminish God's power or to deprecate God's ability to work miracles. It is meant to see God's power and miracles operating mostly in quiet and undramatic ways visible more to religious faith than to ordinary unaided human senses. This is due in part to a marveling at the astounding genius in the workings of the created and human order and to feeling esteem through the exercise of analytical intelligence.

Such marveling and esteem are often accompanied by a heightened sense of the wisdom of the Creator who accomplishes designs slowly and methodically through the processes of the nature that has been God's doing. Responding to the Bible in this frame of mind, the critical interpreter is typically prone to favor evidence that the biblical depiction of certain miracles or spectacular divine tours de force are probably more the work of the inspired authors' imagination than of their memory or knowledge of historical events. Critical interpreters can respect these imaginative accounts, for such stories may reveal to them that the events are God's special work, that the events portrayed would otherwise not have happened and are thus in this sense wondrous or miraculous.

The wonderment of the critical interpreter is then of a different kind than that of the fundamentalist interpreter. It is more influenced by the activity of the left brain and is, therefore, more analytic and conceptual. Such a response results in a faith whose activities and attitudes have been carefully examined according to the criteria that the critical interpreter finds valid and that appear in this perspective to lend greater respectability to the interpretation (McKnight, 48).

The reliance on modern criteria of judgment may, for the critical interpreter, be particularly important in certain areas of ethics. For the Bible contains many directives that, for the age and culture in which they were written, can be perceived today as overtly or by implication recommending such conventions as tribalism, slavery, vindictiveness, sexism, ethnic elitism, and anti-Semitism (Spong, 16–22). Even a fundamentalist interpreter can be flexible enough to ignore many such norms or to disclaim their continued relevance. For critical interpreters, however, forms of analysis that more extensively appear to accord with modern scholarly analysis may facilitate such disclaimers.

Scientifically Sound

If objective conditions justify absolutizing the critical interpretation of the Bible, it is as if God is inviting believers to involve in their faith the knowledge, judgments, and dispositions that have been typically nurtured in persons of the modern scientific age. Here, the religious system includes inferences showing an expectation that divine and human conduct accord in large measure with divinely created human reason (Proverbs 2:2–6; 1 Corinthians 2:16). In such a context, the use of the mind can be understood as an element of giving praise to God (Spong, x).

General Risks of Absolutizing

Falsely Secure

It has been maintained here that, theoretically, the absolutizing of a single religious system could be correct. This amounts to saying that, in principle, the fundamentalist and critical interpreters' respective absolutizing of their systems could be right, at least with regard to their invariable elements, features that are essential to their definitions as specific systems. But because of the apparent limitations of knowledge influenced by faith (namely, all knowledge, by the terms of this discussion), it also amounts to saying how presumptuous it might be to declare one of the systems wrong, or how hasty it might be to deny the possibility of the divine's full identification with a single religious system. Presumption and haste of these kinds thus exemplify the fallacy of Christian certitude. Maybe there really is only "one fish in the sea"; maybe there is not. There appears to be no way to know with an objective certainty that excludes belief or faith.

A forceful argument has been made that, by the views of certain "reformed epistemologists" of the analytical tradition in philosophy, the fundamentalist interpreters' faith cannot be demonstrated conclusively to be any less valid than any other since the fundamentalist approach to the Bible appears as one basic form of authentic religious belief among many (Tilley, 237–38, 246–47). While these philosophers follow a very different course than the one we are following here, their inference bears strong resemblances to an evaluation of the fundamentalist approach from a systems perspective. Here, however, the same conclusion is drawn regarding critical interpretation of the Bible. In other words, both approaches to Scripture theoretically appear, in their essential and invariable features, as elements of respectable systems of religiousness.

It has also been intriguingly contended that, from a Heideggerian philosophical perspective that highlights Western thought's tendencies to absolutize or seek objective certainty, the fundamentalist approach appears to be fulfilling its destiny, namely, to be following a natural course determined by a given context in the history of being (O'Connell). As persuasive as this contention may be, from a systems perspective a similar judgment seems advisable regarding critical interpretation. Both approaches to the Bible appear to have become distinct currents of interpretation in the history of Western thought, in which philosophy, theology, and other sciences have contributed to a tendency to absolutize. When

characterized by an assumption that faith has given rise to totally
objective certainty, this tendency fuels the fallacy of Christian certitude.

The recognition that any absolutizing involves an act of faith
appears to elicit respect for the possible rightness of alternate viewpoints that are defended as compellingly as one's own has been.
There is always the possibility that the perception of another
person's meaning system as erroneous or deficient is merely a projection of error or deficiency one unconsciously senses or fears in
one's own, despite a commitment of faith. To avoid projecting onto
another, one must apparently be willing to doubt even one's most
cherished presuppositions and to subject them to careful scrutiny.
It is something like removing a large irritant from one's own eye
before attempting to remove a minute irritant from the eye of someone else (Matthew 7:5). Such self-examination entails humble self-
regard and the knowledge that projection can lead to unjust deg-
radation of others, a situation that breeds further mistrust and
separation (Jung, *Self,* 114–17).

Complacent

There thus appear to be good theoretical reasons for remaining
open about the finality of the truth one perceives within a system.
But there appear as well to be good practical reasons. First of all,
as most scientists, theorists, or teachers will admit, the "truth" is
seemingly so great that it cannot be encapsuled in pat concepts or
formulas. So even if one's system is objectively the truest, one can
always grow in the understanding that it brings. Even if one's beloved is the one sent by heaven, one cannot assume to know him
or her entirely; such knowledge, if attained at all, typically takes a
lifetime of commitment and dialogue. It is apparent here that meaning systems can be tenuous, not only because their varying elements allow something to be understood in various ways, but also

because, as open systems, they allow an eventual observation that what was originally understood contained an excess of meaning that has been grasped only later (Johnson, 151).

Reflecting on the elements of their general religious system, most Christians could agree, for example, that they are constantly learning more about the role and meaning of Christ in their lives, even as they understand that the fullness of Christ has always been available for them; there was in him an excess as a fullness they did not originally grasp. Likewise, most Christians could claim that there is and will long be much that they can learn from the Bible. Being consistent, they might do well also to agree that they have much to learn about their notions of how to interpret the Bible.

Haughty

It would seem to be presumptuous, if not self-righteous, for Christians to claim that they are fully in accord with what God wants from them. And since the truth of the system in which they live may be tenuous, it seems similarly presumptuous to deny the value, even the possibility of the supreme value, of alternate elaborations within the general Christian system. If it is possible that one's particular system contains much truth but is still tainted with some blindness and error, it could be conversely possible that an alternate system that one perceives to be tainted by much blindness and error still contains much truth. And that truth, however unappealing, may still be worth preserving. In the first chapter of Philippians, Paul shows no fear of a Christian party he opposes, for he sees that even such an opponent contributes to the spread of the gospel.

Even if it is true that one's differentiated religious system or one's religious subsystem is objectively the best, the value of making that claim can easily be diminished by the implication that alternate particular systems are considerably inferior. For the value of absolute commitment lies in a fidelity that is constantly renewed by deepened fervor and keener understanding. Even as wholesome closeness with persons other than the beloved can nurture an abiding commitment to the beloved, so an enriching exposure to other differentiated variants of one's system or even to other general religious systems would seem to be able to nurture one's commitment to one's own interpretive religious system. Many Christians have grown firmer in the understanding and practice of their faith because of respectful ecumenical dialogue with non-Christians. Among these same Christians, ironically it would seem, there has been adamant rejection of positions assumed by others within the Christian fold. When this happens between fundamentalist and critical interpreters of the Bible, they likely forgo an opportunity to deepen their respective commitments while still learning from one another.

Absolutizing thus appears to have its merits and its risks. The merit seems to lie in the commitment, security, and—if the system should be of supreme value—rightness that ensue. Some support then can be given to the tendencies of Christians to absolutize their respective cultures of belief, whether they do so in fundamentalist or critical ways. Yet such absolutizing does not appear to be without its risks, among which may be self-righteousness, projection, narrow-mindedness, and stifled growth in the faith. These are traits that critical interpreters frequently attribute to fundamentalist interpreters (Russell, 217), but from which critical interpreters themselves do not appear to be immune.

Closed-Minded

Such traits can be particularly harmful when taken in connection with attitudes or actions in the areas of morality and politics. One need not deny the universality of some moral imperatives to observe that some claims to absolute certainty about what is right or wrong can lead to policies, institutions, or procedures that are harmful to individuals, races, nations, or humanity generally. For example, convictions of certainty regarding certain implications of the right to life, no matter what the medical conditions of a given pregnancy, can result in injustice to either the born or unborn. Likewise, convictions of certainty regarding social or political institutions can prolong or foment undue suffering and persecution. Such convictions are often variable features within a differentiated religious system and are thus subject to change without dismissing the system as such.

Often, the absolutizing of principles within a system results in a failure or refusal to appreciate the view that decisions as to what is best frequently need to be arrived at through a long and sometimes painful process of weighing the issues (Tracy, 91, 95) in light of legal and ethical traditions, religious teachings, careful reasoning, discerning intuition, compassion, and common sense—all of which may impinge on another weighing factor, one's preferred interpretation of relevant biblical texts. Both critical and fundamentalist interpreters of the Bible can be narrow in this way, forgetting how flexible their own systems can be, or dismissing one another's interpretive systems in a wholesale way and thus driving one another into a fiercer absolutizing of their entire systems. The intense polarization between Christians that can ensue from the issues pertaining to the unborn or the socio-economic situation in developing countries may be cited as examples of this. There may be compelling reasons for ferocity in the face of the opposition. But the risk of self-righteous absolutizing in the process is quite great.

All of these risks, however, plus others, appear with greater clarity when examined with specific reference to each of the two systems in question.

Risks of Fundamentalist Interpretation

Superficial

By its close association with right-brain functions, fundamentalism gains a vibrancy that is characteristic of emotive and image-laden forms of awareness. Many fundamentalist interpreters, for example, accept that Jesus literally walked on water; so they may marvel at a miraculous intervention of God in which is manifest to them the direct revelation of God's power over nature. Their vibrant perception of this power is immediate and secure. By the same token, however, they risk sacrificing cogency and persuasiveness by undue concomitant diminishment of left-brain functions. The cogency meant here comes from the kind of understanding associated with calculative and rational investigation. Reflection and analysis of varying kinds give such understanding a unique power to judge, reason, and make appropriate applications. The persuasiveness comes from the frequently greater appeal that reasoned and scientific awareness have in an age where such knowledge is highly valued. Where unrelenting certainty appears bereft of something like cogency or persuasiveness, reflections on texts or ideas can seem repetitive and boring (Tracy, 101).

Out of Touch

Discussing the life setting in which the walking-on-water stories (for example, Matthew 14:22–33) were originally recounted, probing the expectations of audiences in such a milieu, or examining the literary form of the story in light of the overall plan of the author can lead to a diminished sense of literalness. For many today this is a welcome sense; their faith is more enhanced by it than burdened, for they feel that they have a faith that is more respectable for having answered to the appropriate demands of reason. Many students of the Bible, for example, find more credibility in asserting that a faith-filled author or community wrote or responded to a basically metaphorical account of Jesus' and thus God's power than in unassumingly accepting that such dramatic interruptions of God's own physical laws occurred.

If fundamentalist interpreters examine some scholarly findings such as those just mentioned and still retain a heightened sense of literalness, it may be because they still diminish left-brain activity by not considering the critical questions regarding their own assumptions about the nature of biblical truth. This too leaves them out of touch and thus lacking cogency for those who expect that such issues should not be taken for granted (Noll, 148).

Here, when dealing with the risks of the fundamentalist approach, we are not speaking of need as much as expediency. For their own faith and for the faith of many others whom they want to inspire, the present fundamentalist perspective seems clearly sufficient. What they perhaps should ask, though, is whether this view is worth the price of neglecting some of the most notable advances of the natural sciences, of the humane and social sciences, and of modern human insight. If such advances can be seen to reflect something of God's loving concern that all children of God advance in wisdom, then perhaps the cost is too great. If, on the other hand, certain advances of these kinds are perceived as modernistic (Ammerman, 76) or even as the work of the devil, then the fundamentalist interpreters may have, for better or for worse, firmly entrenched themselves in their own system.

Fearful

Fundamentalist interpreters are noted by many for their inability to compromise (Ammerman, 204). This could, in fact, be what they want, as was discussed earlier in this chapter. Typically, their strategies appear as attempts to preserve a unique social identity that protects them from outside encroachments perceived as ruinous (Marty and Appleby, *Cosmos,* 3). Yet there is a danger in insularity, even if partial. It can be stifling. It can even appear as cultic (Marsden, *Fuller,* 188–89). Exclusivism is not a danger of which fundamentalist interpreters are totally unaware (Falwell, Dobson, and Hindson, 159–63, 179–85). But the danger can bring another risk, fear. Often what one does not know one fears. What is novel or seemingly outlandish can be perceived as threatening or fatal. Fear in the face of a threat can even lead to angry defensiveness (Spong, 5). It can also lead to an uncompromising quest for "power and privilege" over the rest of society or, by fundamentalist leadership, over its own communities (Marty and Appleby, *Glory,* 15–16).

But do fundamentalist interpreters need to be afraid of any challenge from secular theories, modern scholarship, or scientific questioning? Would it not be more profitable for them and all concerned to face such questions with openness and a desire for dialogue? It would seem that the work of spreading faith in Jesus Christ is better served by courage than by fear. If there is nothing too certain of the critical interpreters' conclusions, dialogue could help demonstrate this. In the meantime, there are many who would be repulsed by a Christian faith that appears to have become insular and cultic, cringing before a supposed threat of advances believed by many to be utterly ennobling of the human mind and spirit.

Risks of Critical Interpretation

Irrelevant for Faith

While the conclusions of critical reflection and analysis give an often desired cogency and intellectual look to biblical interpretation, the relevance of such conclusions for faith can be significantly limited. Their relevance lies essentially in their satisfying the need in some Christians' religious systems for a reflective, scientific, or scholarly component; their relevance then is mainly in satisfying a perceived need for a certain kind of faith.

If such satisfaction fulfills a need of what is commonly regarded as authentic religious faith, such faith has been well served. But if this satisfaction is merely or primarily an end in itself, religious faith can be endangered. For example, a conclusion of critical interpretation that can be reached regarding Jesus' calming of the storm (Mark 4:35–41) could be that Jesus never did such a thing historically. If this conclusion is used in the service of a faith that, despite inferences regarding historicity, can nonetheless learn something of, say, God's nature, Jesus' power, the meaning of faith, the laws of nature, or the meaning of fear, then the critical scholar has nurtured not only his or her own faith but the faith of the believing community of Christians as well. But if the conclusion serves only to satisfy, say, a curiosity about whether Jesus in fact did such a thing, it may do nothing for faith at all and may even lead believers to infer that the story is irrelevant.

Overly Heady

In a case like this, the conclusions of critical study can end up satisfying only the needs of other like-minded scholars rather than the needs of a sort of faith that lives and grows in a broader religious community (Wink, *Transformation*, 8–9, 24, 39). Or such conclusions can at least suggest in an elitist way that only one given methodology can appropriately be used to interpret a text; popular interpretations are thus judged as irrelevant (Tracy, 105). The critical method, then, can lead to an undesirable diminishment of right-brain activity (Wink, *Study*, 27) and to considerable insignificance as far as widespread faith is concerned (Towne, 32). And where the critical method becomes a substitute for religious faith as commonly understood, the use of the method can be perceived as an agent of falsehood (Ellis, 418) or even as a form of idolatry (Wink, *Transformation*, 30–31). Rationalism of this kind can represent an impoverishment of the human spirit, namely, a loss of a nearly immeasurable expanse of satisfying and dignifying awareness enjoyed by those who are naturally and unassumingly at home in the world of stories and imagery (Jung, *Memories*, 252–54).

Cumbersome

In being particularly sensitive to the faith response and needs of those who rely on Scripture for religious nurture, a systems approach to certain risks of critical interpretation shares a particular interest with some recent methods of biblical interpretation—for example, feminist interpretation, reader-response criticism, narrative criticism, and canonical criticism (Keegan; Tate)—that find limits to exclusively historical-critical approaches to the Bible (McKnight). For, like the aforementioned methodologies, a systems approach to biblical interpretation is markedly concerned with the *text's audience,* namely, the hearers or readers in their reception, appropriation, or use of the sacred text. The historical-critical method, which still dominates in contemporary biblical scholarship, focuses largely on the author/editor and the *text's background*—for example, on the sources, setting, vocabulary, and objectives that influenced the composition of Scripture in its present form. Still other interpretive methodologies of a literary-critical sort emphasize the importance of the *text itself.* Nonetheless, the established and emerging methodologies all to some degree overlap, so that certain assumptions and issues of one can usually be found in at least one of the others. An interpreter can thus feel drawn to the cumbersome task of mental juggling in order to appear respectably critical. Insofar as all such interpretive methodologies share the general tendency to contrast with a fundamentalist interest in literalism, the risks of critical interpretation as discussed here are attributable to them all.

Elitist

For critical scholars, the preference for a specific kind of scholarly component can be so strong that they may judge their method of interpretation to be the superior one (Inbody, 89). This, as observed in chapter 1, is a tendency of any absolutizing. But in a scientific age, what appears to be unscientific is easily subject to belittling. A critical interpretation can thus easily lead to smugness, a kind of arrogance that can well compete with whatever insularity may appear from the fundamentalist side. The risks of the critical method then appear to be real and grave.

Summary

The tendency to absolutize one's religious system is typically accompanied by the tendency to deny that one has absolutized in a purely subjective way. If absolutizing includes the assertion that other systems are not this system's equivalent, one can become locked into a given system and become unamenable to any other. Theoretically, a given religious system could be absolutely and objectively the best. Since every claim is made within a system accepted in some kind of faith—be it religious or nonreligious faith—there appears to be no purely objective certainty whereby one could absolutely discount claims to absolute truth. A Christian's claim to such certainty constitutes the fallacy of Christian certitude. Therefore, it seems reasonable to be sympathetic enough with the claims of both fundamentalist and critical interpreters to consider at least some assets of each system.

The fundamentalist approach is clear and unencumbered. Involving a childlike directness and exuberance, it involves an unambiguous acceptance of the supernatural and a unique and very strong element of right-brain activity. The critical interpretation of the Bible has strong appeal in a scientific age. In submitting the elements of its faith processes to research and reason in its particular ways, this approach demonstrates great respect for science and the laws of the natural order understood in the Christian system to be created by God.

Yet absolutizing cultures of belief has risks, not the least of which are complacency, self-righteousness, projection, and narrow-mindedness. Risks that can be specifically associated with the fundamentalist approach include lack of cogency, diminished persuasiveness in an age in which the effects of left-brain activity are highly regarded, insularity, and fear. In a similar way, absolutizing a critical interpretation risks diminished right-brain activity, arrogance, irrelevance for religious faith, and the diminishment or nullification of religious faith.

Chapter 4

The Potential of Mutual Recognition

Renewed Dedication

Your Position Is Respectable

Thus far we have observed that the tension between the fundamentalist and critical interpreters can be related to their respective attachments to their religious meaning systems. The sense of well-being that each group receives through the mediation of its system can be perceived to be based primarily on the significance of the five main elements of the Christian system. The elements so designated are Jesus Christ, his Cross, his

Resurrection, the Church, and the Bible. The sense of absolute meaning that such attachment brings is in each group often accompanied by an absolutizing of the differentiated Christian system, that is, of their specific systems insofar as they include the five main elements as well as all other differentiations, including the particular elements of either the fundamentalist or the critical approach to the Bible. Since principles of interpretation as discussed in this book seem to grant that, in theory, any religious absolutizing may be true, at least as far as invariable features are concerned, the claims of each system appear to merit careful and sympathetic attention. Yet in each case there seem to be risks, both for individual faith and for the cause of Christianity as a whole.

In the interest of an ever-growing Christian faith, then, it seems advisable not to absolutize in either case. The two cultures of belief thus appear as tenable. This does not necessarily mean that either side must relinquish its firm commitment to the system in which it finds great satisfaction. Nor does it necessarily mean that either side must be enthusiastic about the other system. The hesitance to absolutize would, along with an attempt to avoid the fallacy of Christian certitude, simply mean mutual recognition. At a minimum, in the interest of faith, such recognition would mean the respectful tolerance of one another's systems as legitimate systems of Christian religiousness. Ideally, it would seem to mean the mutual acceptance of one another's systems as at least equal (Lines, 155–57) or—remaining true to the principles of interpretation spoken of in the last chapter—as possibly even superior.

In the last chapter, Paul's own tranquillity in the face of an opposing Christian faction was observed. In Philippians 2, he exhorts his readers not only to rid themselves of contentiousness but even, with a humble assumption regarding the opponent's possible superiority, to follow Christ's example and serve the opponent's needs. The extent to which such an ideal is realized would, it seems, depend on the extent to which both sides could recognize in one another firm and authentic reliance on the main elements of the Christian system. In other words, the range of attitudes between mere tolerance and full acceptance of one another's systems would depend on the degree to which each side could appreciate the other's religiousness as a true form of Christianity. This does not have to mean appreciating it as a perfect form of Christianity or as one whose variable features in no way need to change.

Your Position Is Admirable

Many Christians, if not the majority, recognize generally that most forms of Christian religiousness—especially the main branches, denominations, or rites—are legitimate. They recognize that the Christian faith lived in the context of the wide variety of elaborated religious systems is authentic. To doubt the firmness of faith in these circumstances could be to doubt the integrity of most of one's fellow Christians; and that would require an uncommon cynicism. The valuing of alternate forms of Christianity is at minimum a way of granting the functional importance of Christianity in the distinctive lives and varying cultures of millions of people; here, in other words, Christianity is perceived to be doing much good, both religiously and socially; people's lives and the world they live in are viewed as better off for such faith.

The recognition of such authenticity in faith is based, it seems, on an at least implicit recognition of the primacy of major elements of the Christian religious system. In earlier chapters it was mentioned that because of what are here being called the "five main elements" of Christianity, Christians worldwide can distinguish themselves as a group vis-à-vis other religions of the world. The number five was not necessarily meant to be definitive; surely there are alternate ways to elucidate what is of main importance in

Christianity. The point is, though, that at least some elements must be perceived as primary, and other elements must be perceived as secondary. If this were not the case there would be no sense of some kind of solidarity among Christians within the multiple differentiated systems, and there would be no ecumenical efforts to seek more formal unity in a body perceived, however vaguely, to be essentially one Church.

In Different Ways, the Bible Unites Us in Faith

A clear variant among the elements of the multiple differentiated Christian systems is the method of biblical interpretation. The varying positions on this matter distinguish Christian denominations from one another and, as has been observed in chapter 1, further distinguish local churches within denominations and groups or individuals within local churches. Since this variation has by and large not been enough to negate a general sense of the overriding identity of Christianity as a worldwide religion, the matter of biblical interpretation would appear to be a minor element compared to the five under discussion here.

This is understandable in light of the nature of Christian faith understood as first and foremost an interpersonal matter. This means that according to most Christians, their faith is a matter of personal commitment to and relationship with a personal God and God's personal saving presence through Jesus Christ. Biblical teachings about God and Jesus Christ are surely important for this faith; they depict the dispositions of those toward whom faith is directed. All such dispositions may not be regarded as equally important; and none of them are thought to be as important as God and Jesus Christ in themselves. For example, it appears to be more important to believe in God who is the creator and the faithful partner of the covenant than to believe that all, some, or none of the biblical depictions of God's creativity and fidelity are historical. Likewise, it appears to be more important to believe in Jesus Christ as the human incarnation of God's saving love than to believe that all, some, or none of the biblical depictions of his humanity and love are historical. In other words, personal saving faith seems to be more important than some of the beliefs that are related to it. Thus biblical interpretation, to the extent that it leaves intact the general unanimity regarding the five main elements of Christianity, appears to be of secondary importance in the Christian belief system, even in the variety of synthesizing systems within the general system.

If this is so, then there would seem to be good reasons for fundamentalist and critical interpreters to appreciate one another's types of faith as valuable and authentic. As long as they can see in one another's cultures of belief a true commitment to the risen Jesus Christ, as long as they can accept his life and death as part of God's design for saving them all and thus constituting them all as the Church, and as long as they can find in the Bible the witness of their common salvation, they would seem to do well to rejoice in their unity. This is apparently an important part of what they are doing when from differing perspectives they can nurture one another in Bible-study groups, support one another in times of major crises, or minister to one another in other times of need. Their differences appear to be insignificant in the practical realm, namely, as far as Christian life, love, and ministry are concerned.

We Serve Different Needs

Yet they would also seem to do well to rejoice in certain differences. For their differing ways of interpreting the Bible correspond to differing religious needs. Fundamentalist interpreters thrive in their faith through their acceptance of the literal truth of most of God's or Jesus' wondrous deeds as recounted in the Bible. Critical interpreters thrive in their faith through a nurtured sensitivity to the many perceived literary forms in which such stories appear to be recounted. The needs of the two groups are different, not respecting the relationship with God or Jesus Christ, but respecting the way the relationship is understood and fostered.

In a situation such as this, mutual recognition means that the parties in each system recognize the value of their respective cultures in a way that avoids the fallacy of Christian certitude. They have, in other words, a sense of absolute meaning without a sense of totally objective truth, at least insofar as they are differentiated Christian systems being compared with one another. As Christian systems vis-à-vis other religions of the world they may be absolutized by some in either group. But as already mentioned, the appropriateness of this kind of absolutizing will be discussed in the final chapter. Vis-à-vis one another, they neither exclude one another nor rate one another as inferior.

At the same time, though, each group can remain by and large content with its own system. A recognition of alternatives does not need to mean the abandonment of one's position. It can, in fact, lead to a renewed appreciation of one's position as contrasted with another. Fundamentalist interpreters may, for example, be pleased that critical interpreters are contributing to the nurturance of the Christian faith and that their own approach to the Bible is a greater help to those whose faith would be burdened by numerous distinctions and an apparent lack of clarity. They can rejoice, then, in their view's greater practicality for a large number of people (Ashcraft, 538). Critical interpreters, on the other hand, might be pleased that the fundamentalist approach meets so many people's needs and that their own approach to the Bible can help answer questions that are sometimes a burden to faith. They can rejoice too, namely in their view's greater practicality for a sizeable number of believers. Each group then can approach its religious system with a sense of renewed dedication, with a sense that this system is valuable, both to themselves and to the others, and that this diversity is enriching Christianity.

Renewed Togetherness

Seeing Things in a Fresh Way

A movement toward mutual recognition would bring to fundamentalist and critical interpreters a certain change that may not at once be noticed. For the sympathy of the groups for one another's systems, along with a renewed dedication of each group to its own system, would bring about in each group a new disposition toward its own system. Such a disposition can be likened to a state of what, in discussions regarding response to symbols, has been called "second naiveté."

A symbol can communicate its meaning without any reflective interpretation or understanding on the part of the respondent or beholder. This response is termed "primitive naiveté." On the other hand, one can lose communication with a symbol by interpreting it according to preconceptions not intended for the symbol. For example, one can accept a story as literally true and be accordingly impacted by it, or one can allegorize the story—that is, interpret its symbols in ways that may in fact be foreign to the story's purpose. In second naiveté, however, one is affected by the immediacy of the symbolism and at the same time involved in a creative and reflective understanding of its meaning (Ricoeur, *Symbolism*, 350–55, and *Conflict*, 298–300).

The same can be said when symbolism functions on the larger scale of myth, namely of story, whether historical or not, that communicates profound truths, especially those of a religious nature. In primitive or "first" naiveté, the respondent or believer accepts the symbol or myth spontaneously and immediately while being

drawn toward the truth that is being expressed. Later comes awareness of a cognitive kind, bringing concepts that may be articulated philosophically or theologically. This intermediate phase,
however, while quite valuable for evaluating what was first experienced, "destroys" the immediacy of the original meaning. The
second naiveté that follows is thus "restorative" in that it allows
the recipient or believer to evaluate consciously what was accepted
in the first and intermediate phases. Through such consciousness
one may enjoy a transformed relationship to the sacred (Klemm,
69–73).

Critical or reflective distance from a religious symbol, which in
other contexts has been called "demythologizing," can provide
needed clarification and evaluation of the symbol. But unless such
distancing—something more typical of critical interpretation than
of the fundamentalist approach—is accompanied by some form of
"remythologizing," or fresh presentation of the original experience of the symbolism, the religious symbol loses its unique power
to mediate divine transcendence (Nielsen, 154–57).

In second naiveté, there is a different kind of openness to the
symbol, a kind of acceptance that includes much of the directness
and innocence of the original naive acceptance of the symbol. And
the reflective distancing from the story has not diminished the
intended impact of it (Fowler, 187–88, 197). Second naiveté, then,
is a "mature innocence" whereby biblical texts can be adopted or
appropriated in a new way (Wallace, 52, 56–60). And because the
texts are uniquely important in their specific communication of
religious teaching, interpretation of them can be properly theological, part of the activities and dispositions of a believing community, and not merely articulations of some general religious sense
(Poland, 183) like a philosophical understanding of religion. Second naiveté is thus able to bridge a gap that can emerge between
the Bible and critical interpretation of it so that the sacred text's

original impact, understood in terms of faith, may be restored (Peters, 280).

For example, one may have heard the story of the good Samaritan (Luke 10:30–35) and, presuming it to be historical, been impressed that such a kind man once performed such an admirable deed on behalf of the injured man from Jerusalem. The Samaritan may have served as a historical model of virtue. Later, one may learn that the story is one of Jesus' parables and, therefore, that its historicity is unlikely. The disappointment that may follow this discovery could lead to a feeling of estrangement from the story, to a sense that the story's symbolic power—namely, its power to communicate truth—has been lost. The estrangement from its symbolism might be carried further if one exchanges one's naive acceptance of the story for an allegorical interpretation in which, say, the characters represent personalities of the Church in Europe during later centuries. On the other hand, an acceptance of the story's fictional nature can be accompanied by a considerate reflection on what the story communicates, say about love, neighborliness, or Jesus Christ's own kind of compassion. Such new and reflective openness to the immediacy of the symbolic impact of the story could be understood as an instance of second naiveté.

A New Approach to One's Belief System

One's meaning system can be approached in a parallel way. One can live within a system and never reflect on its influence in facilitating a perception of truth. Or one can reflect on the influence of a system and still accept it as a given and beyond question. But one can also—by way of system theory, hermeneutics, deconstructionism, or some other method—learn to draw out more implications of one's system and of alternate systems. This can lead to respect for alternate meaning systems and even to confusion or disillusionment as to any system's degree of rightness. But it can also lead one back to one's own system by means of second naiveté.

For fundamentalist and critical interpreters it is a case of one differentiated Christian system or subsystem as an alternate to another. Persons in each group may begin with a certain "naiveté" regarding their respective systems of interpretation. Persons in each group may unquestioningly presume their system to be the best or even the sole authentic system of religiousness, Christian or otherwise. In other words, individuals in each group may have absolutized their system. Having examined one another's systems, however, and having granted one another recognition of the type being discussed here, their dispositions toward their respective systems would no longer be characterized by the original "naiveté." Rather, having accepted that absolutizing is highly problematic and possibly counterproductive for Christianity's goals, each would have introduced a component that may not have been present or explicit before.

Each group then would have made a kind of sacrifice, the sort of abandonment, transition, and renewal that usually involves pain (Fowler and Keen, 138). Each group—for the good of itself, the other group, and Christianity in general—would have given up its original "naiveté" regarding its system. This sacrifice need not lead to abandonment of one's system but, as noted above, can lead to renewed dedication to it. For both groups, such dedication would involve second naiveté. Persons in both groups would profit from the special authentic insights that faith in their respective systems brought them in the first situation of "naiveté." In second naiveté, their systems would function as a religious symbol does; for such a symbol is part of a complex of elements that communicate the divine or absolute (Ricoeur, *Conflict*, 12, 319). Their systems, then, must likewise be accepted in faith, not in "naive" or unreflective faith, but in the kind of simple immediate faith on which the fair and honest reflection on a symbol's meaning must rely (Ricoeur, *Conflict*, 389–90).

Willingness to Reform

Should the sacrifice of original "naiveté" in fact involve the sacrifice of something erroneous or undesirable among the system's variable elements, it would mean something like the death of an idol, the kind of death that is necessary so that what is being communicated may be more fully understood (Ricoeur, *Conflict*, 467). If the system through which second naiveté is reached is itself a means of more clearly knowing religious truth, the possible deficiencies of variable elements within the original system of biblical interpretation may become more evident. This would be insight that the proponent and the opponent of the original interpretive methods should welcome equally. Thus in the mutual recognition of second naiveté, in the mutual entry into a new state of openness, persons in both groups would enjoy a new solidarity. Their previous unity as members of the worldwide Church would be enhanced not only through a new kind of critical dialogue but also through a new solidarity of mutual respect and encouragement, of renewed faith in all that they together hold as sacred.

Practical Unanimity

"As If" We Share

A situation of renewed dedication and togetherness for fundamentalist and critical interpreters might allow for another, perhaps more powerful, dimension of unanimity. This would pertain to the similarities that could arise from the critical interpreters' new recognition of the fundamentalist interpreters' preference for claiming the literalness of biblical stories and directives. For persons in the fundamentalist group, the sacrifice for the sake of renewed togetherness in second naiveté would involve giving up a "naive" disposition that leads to absolutizing their preference. The sacrifice would thus involve a willingness to admit a new element into whatever critical disposition has been present with regard to literalness. For persons in the critical group, the sacrifice for the sake of renewed togetherness in second naiveté would involve giving up a "naive" disposition that leads to absolutizing the preference for claiming a larger number of interpretations that significantly limit the amount of literalness in the Bible. Here too the sacrifice would involve a willingness to admit a new element into whatever critical disposition has been present with regard to literalness.

The difference in this new element for the two groups may be said to be this: for the fundamentalist interpreters, it is the element of theoretical openness regarding literalness or normativeness perceived to be but that might not be; for critical interpreters, it is the element of theoretical openness regarding literalness or normativeness perceived not to be but that might be. The fundamentalist interpreters would be responding to most biblical accounts, not in original but in second naiveté, as if the fundamentalist interpretive system is the most appropriate for faith. In their original naiveté, *as if* meant by and large concluding unquestioningly. In second naiveté, *as if* means clearly concluding critically and appreciating the value and possible limits of concluding unquestioningly. The critical interpreters would be responding to many biblical accounts, not in original but in second naiveté, *as if* the critical interpretive system is the most appropriate for faith. But in *their* original naiveté, *as if* meant concluding for the most part questioningly. In second naiveté, *as if* means appreciating the value and possible limits of concluding questioningly; it means questioning the tendency to absolutize even their own original questioning disposition.

For example, in original naiveté, fundamentalist interpreters may have concluded unquestioningly that the creation accounts in Genesis are factual. In second naiveté, because they are open to the possibility that their conclusions may not be absolute, they would not be disturbed by another's critical conclusion that the accounts are not factual. In original naiveté, critical interpreters may have concluded questioningly that the same creation accounts are not factual. In second naiveté, because they concede the possibility that their conclusions may not be absolute, they would not be disturbed by a fundamentalist conclusion that the accounts really are factual. Clearly, there would be unanimity between the two groups, at least of a negative sort. For neither side would be disturbed by what the other side denies. It would be at least a situation of "live and let live."

Attaining such togetherness would likely be more problematic in areas where the literalness of biblical texts means the binding character of moral injunctions. For it is one thing to recognize the possibility that a story may be factual or not. But it is another thing to recognize the possibility that a given moral directive may be binding or not. Where more may be at stake than personal preferences in interpretation, where the interests of other persons may likely be impacted through actions rooted in moral decisions, acceptance of diversity can be much more challenging. Here, great delicacy on both sides would be in order. And the upshot of second naiveté here might or might not be a negative unanimity of one side's not rejecting what the other denies. Whatever the case, at least it can be hoped that an introduction of second naiveté into the relationship would have opened channels of communication that were likely not present before.

Imagine That

But the critical interpreters' openness to the value of the fundamentalist preference for literalness could lead to unanimity of a clearly positive kind if they could find *practical* value in responding to most biblical stories as if they were factual. The suggestion that they join fundamentalist interpreters in approaching the Bible in second naiveté—thus acting as if their respective interpretations are correct—allowed for *theoretical* unanimity in critically admitting the possibility of the other's correctness. There, the *as if* meant *critical reservation* about one's own system of interpretation and allowed for a negative unanimity of no longer denying that the other could be right. But if the *as if* would mean *imagining,* the critical interpreters would enter into an affirming practical unanimity with fundamentalist interpreters by recognizing the value of imagining most biblical accounts as literally true. The fundamentalist interpreters would imagine this because they have concluded in original and second naiveté that this is so. The critical interpreters would be imagining this because they have concluded in second naiveté that this is valuable. Criteria for such valuing can be found, at least in part, among the interpretive methods of redaction criticism, a literary-critical approach that is much relied upon in historical-critical approaches to Scripture (Morgan and Barton, 212–13).

One aim of redaction criticism is to interpret texts in light of the author's or final editor's presumed or demonstrated plan and purpose for the given work (Krentz, 51–52). The author or editor will be referred to here as the writer.

In the Gospel of Matthew, for example, the stories about Jesus' confrontation with the Pharisees might be interpreted in light of the writer's overall plan to demonstrate the gradual revelation of the kingdom that occurs in conjunction with Jesus' preaching and mission. According to such an interpretation, this gradual unfolding of the divine plan might for the writer be relevant to the mission of the Church after Jesus' death and Resurrection. Therefore, the writer's purpose in this gospel would be to recount Jesus' ministry in a way that especially speaks to the situation of the post-Resurrection Church. What the writer says of Jesus, then, is likely colored, at least in part, by the needs of that Church. Here, the perspectives of the redaction critic may be said to overlap with the concerns of the narrative critic. For what the former sees as the author's purpose in light of the Church's perceived needs, the latter may see in terms of the "implied reader" (Tate, 75), namely, the audience for whom the text appears to be intended.

One of the needs of this fledgling Church was to hold its own in certain quarters against the resistance of contemporary Diaspora Judaism, the Judaism that had gained a footing about the Mediterranean and Middle Eastern world due to the scattering of Israel after the exile and later after the fall of Jerusalem. Such resistance would have typically come from that group of Jews who had largely been responsible for Israel's survival, namely the Pharisees. It was this group, more perhaps than the Pharisees of Jesus' own times, with which the gospel writer is at odds—or so the interpretation might go. In the time of the writer's Church, Israel too was struggling for survival, something that was less true during the time of Jesus, despite the powerful presence of Rome that loomed over all. Thus, a redaction or historical critic might say that the historicity of the confrontation scenes in this gospel is suspect, at least with regard to their intensity.

One may wonder why, if all of this is true, the writer so distorted history. Actually, the question appears unanswerable as posed. For, coming out of our modern context, it probably relies on standards of accuracy that, as far as we can tell today, had no precise parallel in the writer's time. Israel's method of history-writing shared characteristics of and was influenced by the way other ancient cultures, including those of Greece and several nations of the Near East, approached history (Van Seters, 6–8, 247–48). These ancient historians did not seem to aim for the kind of objectivity for which historians frequently strive today.

Not even among modern historians, though, is there a widespread assumption that they can piece together a fully accurate and objective picture of past events (Trevor-Roper, 1–2). First, all sources on which the historian is dependent are written or retold from a particular, limited, and sometimes biased or erroneous point of view (Kitson Clark, 121). Second, the historian must inevitably select and interpret his or her materials according to certain preferences or biases (Krentz, 35–38, 42–45). Third, it is by use of the imagination, not purely objective scholarship, that the historian assesses significance, namely, by weighing imagined alternatives to events (Trevor-Roper, 20; Stanford, 82–83). And fourth, if the historian sees a certain relevancy to his or her work, the factors that make the work relevant will also impact the way it is fashioned (Smith, 143–47).

Such limits to total objectivity become all the more apparent when one considers some historians' interest in psychological interpretations or imaginative presentations (Elton, 51–87). Historians are thus perceived to "make history" in a very real sense; they fashion accounts of the past, giving their audiences *portraits* of the past that are more like interpretive paintings than like conventional photographs. Such portraits, as models of events no longer available for experience, can be called "*creative* imitations" (Vanhoozer, 96, 192). These constructions are very important for sketching out a perceived past, but their significance is "borrowed" in that it comes from historians' methodologies rather than directly from the historical past. In a paradoxical way, history writing connects readers with the past while breaking from the past;

what has really disappeared appears as retrieved (Ricoeur, *Time,* 1:92, 180; 3:100). And once historians' works are complete, each of their pictures gives varying impressions because of the particular way that each audience or reader interprets them (Stanford, 6, 135, 143–44, 158).

So Imaginative

Nonetheless, the overarching goals of much modern historiography include accuracy and objectivity. So despite the limits of history writing, despite its dependence on records or other accounts that provide mere "traces" of a past that is in many ways removed from our experience, history enjoys a "realistic note" that fictional literature cannot match even if aiming at realism (Ricoeur, *Time,* 1:82). The historian's construction of the past becomes a constellation of referents or descriptors, a system in which the reader can reasonably believe. The reader's acceptance of the historian's communication thus involves faith in a system's connection—indirect as it is—with the past. Learning history thus involves a kind of believing that is inherent in the acceptance of any meaning system. The reader's faith thus joins with the historian's "robust conviction" (Ricoeur, *Time,* 3:142) that the past is being reconstructed. No reputable historian today wants to be accused of undue distortion, prejudice, narrowness, or flights of fantasy. These may be the privileges of the historical novelist but not of the scientific historian (Kitson Clark, 26, 193).

They were, however, the privileges of the ancient historians, as far as we can tell from modern perspectives. Among the ancients, historical recounting, either in speech or in writing, was much more than a means of reconstructing the past; it was as well a means of inspiring, encouraging (Barr, *Scope,* 36, 60, 127), or even entertaining. Stories of a nation's past, particularly of its great leaders, were designed to ennoble the nation, instill pride, nurture hope, and bedazzle the imagination. Such history's worth was judged by the power of its impact (Van Seters, 114, 172, 357). Any flaws would be more those of irrelevance than of a lack of objectivity. The ancient historian's reconstruction of the past was less a verbal reassemblage and more a verbal refashioning. Under such circumstances, historians could have been perceived as distorters of their craft if they had tried to make their accounts of the past too accurate.

For Israel, the greatest hero was the Lord God, and national pride was chiefly a matter of glorifying in God's wondrous deeds on the nation's behalf. Some of the greatest periods of historical creativity in Israel likely occurred during times when national identity and survival required a certain amount of self-assertiveness: during the reign of David in the early decades of the monarchy; amid the struggles of the secessionist northern kingdom; during the Babylonian exile; and during the crucial period of post-exilic reconstruction.

In the judgment of many redaction critics, the historical writings preserved in the Hebrew Scripture, or Old Testament, were fashioned, at least in part, according to the criteria of ancient historical writing (Barr, *Scope*, 13, 37). Israel's history would have served to remind the nation of its origins in God's love and mercy, to nurture thankfulness for God's wondrous intervention on behalf of the chosen people, to caution against complacency in the people's covenant with God, to inspire hope in God's continued protection, and to stimulate expectancy regarding God's ultimate designs for the establishment of a messianic kingdom. The relevance of this history would have lain more in its serving these ends than in its undue meticulousness regarding the details of past events.

The writers of Christian Scripture were still part of a culture in which this style of historiography prevailed. Here, however, the focal point of the heroics was Jesus Christ, and the major glorying was in what God had done to redeem not just a single nation but the entire world. Along with the other evangelists, the writer of the Gospel of Matthew would seem to have had little compunction about adjusting details of his story to suit the gospel's ends and the needs of the Church for whom the gospel was intended. Thus, in critical interpretations such as redaction criticism, mitigated presumptions regarding the literalness of certain stories are regarded as quite acceptable. By such views, in other words, one may legitimately doubt whether all the details of the story are factual.

In chapter 3, the advantages and risks of such critical interpretations of the Bible were explored. It was seen that for some Christians they may be quite helpful. At this point, however, one may well wonder if greater care to respect the biblical writer's intentions might further enhance their helpfulness. With regard to much of the writer's plan and purpose, this respect is already a major element of critical interpretation (Krentz, 40–41; Tate, 174–83). But should not this respect for the writer's expectations regarding the reader or listener be further extended? The biblical writer used various literary forms to proclaim, inspire, encourage, comfort, and challenge. Critical interpreters assert that when such ends involved the use of history, the writer would have reconstructed the past in accord with the usage of the ancients. Would not that usage include both the assumption that the stories would be taken as they are, and the intent that they be accepted and responded to as told or written, that they be imagined to be factual?

Take It Literally

In narrative criticism, answering such a question might be said to involve a reader's getting into an author's story world (Keegan, 113–15). If that world is one in which events should be responded to simply as recounted and not be taken figuratively, say as metaphor or symbolism, would the reader not, according to prescriptions of narrative criticism, do well to take the story literally? Canonical criticism is concerned with the way believers canonized Scripture, namely, received it into Church life when they named the sacred books that made up the Bible. The assumptions, concerns, and goals of the Church that accepted such books are significant elements of canonical criticism's methodology (Tate, 183–85). If Christians of the early centuries of this Church essentially shared the same assumptions about written history as did the biblical authors, biblical editors, and the nonbiblical historians of those ages, should not an interpretation, following the guidelines of canonical criticism, include an acceptance of the literalness of the sacred texts?

Predating an age of modern historiography, the biblical writer would likely never have expected the readers or listeners to theorize regarding the stories' degree of factualness. For achieving its *desired effect,* which was eminently *religious,* the reconstruction of the past was seemingly designed to be accepted simply as rendered. In this spirit and according to common Christian faith assumed to be guided by the Holy Spirit, it was likely that the early Church accepted certain books as the inspired accounts of God's revelation to Israel and, through Jesus Christ, to his Church. These accepted works became the Christian Bible.

In light of the critical interpreter's agility at finding reasons to doubt the literalness of the Bible's stories and norms, it is curious indeed that by some perspectives of redaction criticism (maintaining a respect for the author or editor's intention), narrative criticism (taking account of the implied reader's dispositions), and canonical criticism (considering the assumptions and perspectives of the canonizing Church), arguments in favor of literalness can be suggested. Critical interpreters may thus argue that by and large the Bible's reconstruction of the past should simply be accepted as factual or as literally true and, if such arguments can in a parallel way be applied to directives, that by and large the Bible's moral norms should be accepted as rendered.

Like a reader's belief in the reliability of a historian's reconstruction of the past, acceptance of the biblical text involves faith in the biblical author or editor's account of what is so or what is prescribed. Faith in modern history writing includes sharing the writer's intention that the account be accepted as that of what actually was. Faith in biblical literalness might then include sharing the writer's intention that certain accounts be taken as they stand. In terms of narrative criticism, faith here conforms to the writer's expectations of the implied reader. For Jews and Christians who accept divine inspiration as an element of the writer's work, such faith even becomes an element of religious faith.

Fundamentalist interpreters may rejoice at the direction of such critical interpretation. Except for second naiveté regarding their perspective—that is, except for their employment of literal interpretation *as if* it is the better methodology—they might find themselves fully vindicated by the opposing faction. Critical interpreters, on the other hand, might feel embarrassed by their traditional allies, were it not, however, that their very alliance may in fact be calling them—beyond second naiveté regarding their preferred methodology—toward second naiveté regarding the Bible itself. In other words, in conjunction with the imagination, the scriptural stories and norms would be critically accepted and responded to *as if* they were historically factual or applicable according to their literal meaning.

Here, respect for the writer's intention regarding literal interpretation—a respect attributable to redaction criticism—appears to coalesce with a critical disposition identified with second naiveté, in which a response to the world of the text means a personal "appropriation" of meaning, both an acceptance of the text's own contours of communication and a reflective evaluation of their significance (Poland, 177–78). To enter the world of a narrative is to be affected by its descriptors of reality. Response to a text is thus "the joint work of the text and the reader." Exploring the "movement by which the text unfolds" is thus of prime importance in an interpretative method associated with second naiveté, though attention to the author's intention provides important "guidelines" (Ricoeur, *Time*, 1:76–81).

It is possible, then, for fundamentalist and critical interpreters to find a common ground, to attain an important element of practical unanimity in their basic approaches to the Bible. In such unanimity, fundamentalist interpreters would respond to much of the Bible as if it were historically factual because that is what they take it to be; that is how they imagine it was. Critical interpreters would respond to much of the Bible as if it were historically factual or literally applicable—would imagine it that way—because of some critical methodologies' arguable support for literal interpretation and because they have come to appreciate second naiveté. Since in both cases an *as if* is at play, accord would have been attained.

There is a type of textual interpretation in which an *as if* indicates an assumption of fictitiousness. This means that a text whose facticity is totally denied is interpreted as if it is factual; acceptance of facticity is thus little more than a pretense, though one made for practical reasons. By imagining in second naiveté, however, that a text is factual, the interpreter need not absolutely exclude literalness but essentially demonstrates an appreciation for what is gained in a "naive" acceptance of the text's immediate communication.

For example, a believer could on the one hand pray as if God were a father while holding to a theology that God has no gender whatever. The prayer is said, however, for the practical benefit of sharing with one's religious community or church a certain approach to God. One could imagine, then, that God is male while denying intellectually that this is so. On the other hand, one could pray as if God were a father while suspending absolute judgment regarding God's gender or lack thereof even though one is more disposed to deny that God has any gender. The prayer is said, however, to benefit from a practical acceptance of the literalness of biblical texts that call God a father, that is, while enjoying an image of a father because it communicates something quite precious about God (Vanhoozer, 76–77, 176, 250). Here, then, there is no pretense but joyful and liberating "intersection" between two worlds, namely that of the biblical text and that of the critical reader (Wallace, 70).

The latter procedure would exemplify second naiveté as an element of a critical interpreter's approach to texts. Critical interpreters of the Bible could thus enjoy practical unanimity with fundamentalist interpreters in a positive way, namely, by imagining what literally interpreted texts communicate, by acting as if what the texts say is literally so. Such unanimity goes beyond the rather negative unanimity in which fundamentalist and critical interpreters, not absolutely denying the correctness of one another's interpretive systems, merely act as if their respective methodologies are correct.

As If Jesus Did

Both groups could even find, from their respective positions, an example in the approach to Scripture taken by Jesus, or at least by the writers of the gospels. For the gospels suggest to current interpreters that he accepted much more of the "law and the prophets" as factual than would many critical interpreters today. For example, the gospels suggest that he assumed that David authored

Psalm 110 (for example, Mark 12:36); gospel accounts portray him as implying that Jonah the prophet was a historical figure (for example, Luke 11:29–32); they show him as comfortable with accepting demons as sources of illness and disaster (Luke 13:16; O'Collins, 188–89); they depict him as suggesting that Moses was the author of Exodus 3 (Luke 20:37) and of other parts of Hebrew Scripture (Spong, 23); and they imply that Jesus took literally the Exodus account of Moses' burning-bush experience (Mark 12:26; Boone, 32). On the other hand, in the Gospel of John it is commonplace for Jesus to be misunderstood because his words are taken too literally (for example, 2:20–21, 4:15, 7:34–35, 8:26–27, 11:11–13, 14:4–6, 18:36–38). Practical unanimity regarding literalness need not necessarily, then, be wholesale.

Nonetheless, the harmony induced by mutual second naiveté regarding each group's differentiated Christian system could be enhanced by the critical interpreters' second naiveté regarding the biblical texts themselves. Together, then, the fundamentalist and critical interpreters could reap the advantages of directness and openness vis-à-vis the biblical stories and norms. For example, both groups might respond to the story of Jesus' walk on the water (Matthew 14:22–33) as if it were historically factual; both could reap the benefits of a "naive" acceptance of a story depicting Jesus' power; both could profit from the kind of faith that accepts the revelation of this power as a historical event.

Regarding biblical moral directives, the matter of second naiveté may be less apparent and perhaps more challenging. Accepting norms *as if* they are literally binding might mean appreciating a principle that a norm contains, while with responsibility and discretion appropriately supporting a literal application of the norm in circumstances in which it appears to serve the principle. For example, in the directive that a man's hair should not be long (1 Corinthians 11:14), both fundamentalist and critical interpreters, finding a principle that discernible differences between genders has value for men and women in society and the Church, would submit that men's hair should in fact be shorter than women's when such usage enhances the dignity of both sexes and when contrary usage would offend such dignity.

Working Together

Togetherness and unanimity in fundamentalist and critical interpretation would not necessarily dispel all disharmony between the two groups. Second naiveté may not, in fact, bring total accord to what the two cultures of belief infer from their interpretations. One would not expect all interpretations by persons within a single specific system to harmonize consistently, let alone the interpretations of those in differentiated systems.

Jesus' confrontation with the Pharisees in the Gospel of Matthew is a case in point. Fundamentalist and critical interpreters may respond to the stories as if they are literally true and thus draw from them lessons regarding religious hypocrisy or demeaning religious authoritarianism. With their specific way of accepting such literalness, fundamentalist interpreters may be less prone to diminish the seriousness of Jesus' historical discord with traditional Judaism. In an age of pluralism and ecumenism, their stance can have both advantages (like forthrightness regarding differences between the two religions) and disadvantages (like disrespect between the two religions). And both the advantages and disadvantages could affect the dialogue between Christians and Jews today.

Critical interpreters, on the other hand, while moved because of second naiveté by the force of Jesus' confrontation, may be more prone to diminish the seriousness of it, seeing more perhaps a struggle for survival, first between religious generations but ultimately between parent and child religions. In the Jewish-Christian dialogue, this likewise can have its advantages (like mutual respect and reconciliation) and disadvantages (like patronage from either side). In their dialogue with one another, fundamentalist and critical interpreters who may have generally reached unanimity would have to sort out their remaining differences and decide which conclusions best suit their own needs and those of the whole Church.

The Wider Vision

Here it may become clear that the criteria for the sorting of priorities can well include more than the biblical texts themselves. Nor are disagreements between parties to exegetical rivalry always due to the basic interpretive stances. For example, certain fundamentalist groups may so emphasize other-worldly retribution (an emphasis not inherent to fundamentalist interpretation as such) that immediate concerns for social justice may be minimized. Many see such a minimization prevailing in developing countries. Certain critical interpreters may regard such a stance as promoting injustice. And these critical interpreters appear easily prone to attribute the perceived unjust situation to the fundamentalist approach as such or to call otherworldly interest a typically fundamentalist application of the gospels.

This would seem to be a misnomer, however, since either group might well find enough biblical exhortations to this-worldly responsibility to counter or supplement what it perceives to be a too-narrow indifference by any interpretive approach. This illustrates that any given group, be it fundamentalist or critical, may, rightly or wrongly, expediently or inexpediently, assume a position that could be countered on the basis of its own basic method of biblical interpretation. Inference one way or the other appears to be a matter of preference for certain texts over others, or of concluding that certain texts in certain social situations are more relevant than others. Such conclusions appear to have little to do with a basic interpretive stance (namely, fundamentalist or critical) or seem to be only marginally related to it.

Other conclusions provoking disagreement may indeed be closely linked with basic interpretive positions. These often have to do with moral and social norms. For example, the Bible's references to homosexuals or women may be taken by certain fundamentalist interpreters as literal directives regarding sexual behavior or social roles. Other interpreters may regard the proscribed or prescribed conduct as undue or immoral discrimination in today's world. This, however, provides little warrant for a wholesale rejection of fundamentalist interpretation as such since, as was observed in chapter 1, the fundamentalist approach makes no wholesale claim to the literal truth of *every* biblical statement. Like critical interpretation, the fundamentalist interpretation is free to change or adjust its assessment of a biblical text's literalness and urgency (for example, on the issue of slavery).

Therefore, perceived abuses—which can and do flow from any meaning system, religious or otherwise—should not automatically be attributed to a given interpretive system itself or be regarded as inherent in the system. They may well be variable elements of the system, including its synthesizing systems. Such automatic attribution would be similar to saying that Christians are essentially warmongers because some of them have used the Bible to justify warring that is at a minimum morally questionable. Togetherness and unanimity can be a part of mutual recognition of the parties to the interpretive rivalry without implying that every conclusion within the other's system is acceptable. Debating will need to go on, but not necessarily in terms of the legitimacy of the fundamentalist or critical approaches to the Bible. The rivalry will have to be friendlier, however, requiring more of what Christians call love, something that is the great strength of knowledgeable judgment regarding others' meaning systems (Jung, *Self,* 117–18).

Summary

It would seem that Christianity would greatly profit from the mutual recognition that fundamentalist and critical interpreters might accord one another. Such recognition could vary from mere tolerance to complete acceptance without amounting to either side's relinquishment of its basic approach. Each side, however, would be responding to Paul's exhortation to serve the opposition's need. The key to such accord appears to lie in recognizing the determinative function of the five main elements of the Christian religious system. Since they appear to be primarily what determines whether one's religiousness or faith is Christian, the interpretive method vis-à-vis the Bible would be of secondary import. Which method is used would depend on the religious needs of the interpreter and on the needs of those for whom an interpretation is made. This mutual recognition could bring to each group a sense of renewed dedication within its differentiated system. Such dedication could also bring a renewed sense of togetherness since each culture could find itself in a state of second naiveté regarding its particular belief system.

This togetherness might be further reinforced by a sense of unanimity resulting from the critical interpreters' second naiveté regarding the facticity of many biblical texts. This unanimity, which involves imagining accounts are factual, would appear to accord with the biblical writers' intentions regarding the acceptance of those stories that are presented as historical. A renewed togetherness and practical unanimity of fundamentalist and critical interpreters, a harmony replete with advantages for Christianity, would not, however, be without its challenges to further creative dialogue and accord, particularly with regard to the variable elements in each system.

Chapter 5

Strategies for Teaching or Ministry

Concerns

Meeting Various Needs

Among the challenges accepted by Christianity are growth in the Spirit, the spread of the gospel, and service to those in need. The first pertains to the ever-deepening sense of fulfillment believed to be attainable through the daily practice of faith. The second pertains to continuing attempts to offer others the benefits of such faith. The third involves efforts to help a growing and often hurting world. All of these goals are privileges and responsibilities that effective ministry can help to attain. In that it strives with dispositions of religious faith to enlighten and equip persons for assuming their own rightful places in the Church and world, teaching is included among the Church's many ministries, though in some settings it may rightfully be distinguished from ministry. In the context of this book, teaching may be understood from either viewpoint. Because what follows is a recapitulation and practical application of the book's essential elements, this chapter may be helpful even to those not formally involved in ministry or teaching.

As a form of loving service, ministry is typically believed to be dependent on divine grace, on the generosity of the minister, and on the sensitivity of the minister to the recipient's specific needs. For example, when caring for the terminally ill, the minister can be viewed as God's instrument in exposing the recipient to the comforting and strengthening power of divine love. The minister's generosity in this situation would be seen to mirror something of the generosity of God's continued care. This care can, however, become manifest to the recipient in a variety of ways, perhaps as strength to one who is weak, compassion to one who is in pain, encouragement to one who is despairing, or light to one who faces darkness.

In cooperating with divine grace to provide care in some such way, the minister needs to become informed—usually through dialogue with the recipient—as to where the recipient feels the need and in what sense the recipient relates this need to God or Jesus Christ. The very act of exploring such feelings and empathizing with them is an act of love that can bring the recipient much comfort and spiritual strength. To be fuller, however, this love must be effectively communicated in accord with the recipient's precise area of need. Here, the minister's sensitivity is all-important. Speaking of death, for example, as a transition to greater life can be useless or even alienating to someone who is denying death's approach. Praying for peace and reconciliation can likewise be entirely irrelevant for someone who is angry with God over the prospect of death.

In a similar way, ministers or teachers need to be sensitive to how each person they serve approaches the Bible. It could be alienating to assume unhesitatingly that those of a more critical bent ought to be of a fundamentalist persuasion. For, at least apparently, they have no need to regard many biblical statements as literally true or as normative; this is not part of the system by which their dependence on God and faith in Jesus Christ is mediated. It could be equally inexpedient to presuppose unquestioningly that fundamentalist interpreters need to be molded into a more critical stance; this could risk the violation of their ability to relate to their Lord through a system in which they feel the most satisfaction and comfort. With regard to this issue, then, the minister's or teacher's primary task could be, it seems, to respect each person's preferred interpretation of the Bible, to serve her or him accordingly, and to avoid the fallacy of Christian certitude. This would be consonant with the aims of education generally, and with religious education specifically, to facilitate in students the growth of authentic freedom (Groome, 98). Such an aim could be particularly appropriate in settings in which participants come from various religious backgrounds or have varying dispositions regarding biblical interpretation.

In many situations of ministry or instruction, however, a single approach to Scripture predominates. Perhaps the setting is a denominational one in which it is evident that everyone involved shares similar perspectives. Or, in such settings as classrooms of higher learning, a course may be specifically designed to study sacred texts according to a methodology in which the teacher is an expert. In contexts such as these, ministers or teachers may reasonably and appropriately exclude alternate approaches from discussion.

Opening New Horizons

There appear, however, to be good pastoral or educational reasons for the minister or teacher to modify such a restricted approach at appropriate times. The other needs of those being served, or the broader aims of education, might be weighed against the preferences or immediate goals of those providing service. Ministers or teachers who are parties to exegetical rivalry would then need to accommodate their preferences effectively. Such moments could include those when individuals are discomforted by a particular approach, are merely curious about alternate interpretations, or, sensing limits of the approach at hand, wish to investigate other approaches. There also appear to be times when the minister or teacher should confront individuals or groups with respect to their accustomed interpretations. This would hold no matter which interpretation of the Bible they prefer. In light of a systems approach such as that being taken in this book, the confrontation would not necessarily be designed to change any of them in the direction of a predetermined interpretive system but to facilitate growth in whatever direction and to what extent they are ready.

Such development might mean little more than heightened awareness of the belief system in which an individual is comfortable. But change might also come as movement in the direction of second naiveté, as recognition of an alternate system, as the adoption of an alternate system, or as any workable combination of two or more such alterations. But the minister or teacher would not predetermine any of the directions. One goal in facilitating such change would be to further individual advancement and the growth of the Church. Thus Christianity would be moved in the direction of greater harmony and cooperation in the fulfillment of its mission.

Whatever the outcome, facilitation of change in this area may at times require that the minister or teacher be in some way confrontal. Confrontation has been found to be most helpful when it is caring, respectful, and nondogmatic (Corey, 112–13). In cases involving biblical interpretation, these attributes are eminently applicable. For the minister or teacher would be touching on elements of the individuals' belief systems, elements that are most cherished and that offer a great deal of security. Freedom, therefore, would permeate the atmosphere of this kind of confrontation. Not only does such an atmosphere foster respect for the individuals' rights, it also facilitates change in a most effective manner: few people like to feel forced into a corner. The confronted individuals would feel free to change or not, in whatever direction they choose. And no matter what their choices, each would feel that she or he has the minister's or teacher's respect, something akin to the "unconditional positive regard" (Corey, 253–55) that can be so helpful for communication and personal growth.

Below are several suggestions for pastoral or educational methodologies to deal with alternate approaches to biblical interpretation. These procedures may involve confrontation or may simply be ways of responding to individual needs. The ministries under discussion in this regard would mostly involve preaching, teaching, or catechizing, and those forms of pastoral care that include one-on-one dialogue (for example, hospital ministry, spiritual direction, and pastoral counseling). In sacramental ministry, the issue of biblical interpretation is usually of secondary importance unless there is dialogue involved, as say in Communion for the sick or in reconciliation. Whatever the case, consideration of certain points appropriate to different age-levels or settings can enhance the minister's sensitivity. The methods suggested here resemble the established "shared Christian praxis" approach to religious education (Groome, 184–232). As in that method, the order of the steps is quite variable.

Children

Laying Down the Law

As they learn the difference between right and wrong, children may be cited norms and be given little encouragement to look for exceptions. "You should not steal. Period." This is generally appropriate in their early, formative years. As their ability to reason develops, they may understand the fittingness of exceptions to the rule. "You should not steal, unless perhaps you or someone else is starving to death and there is nothing else you can do." Where parents, or religious communities to which families belong, rely on the Bible for children's moral education, a typical pattern is to cite only those texts that are relevant to the youngsters' levels of maturity and to expect that such scriptural norms will be taken literally. In this area, then, there would seem to be little need to distinguish between fundamentalist and critical interpretations of biblical texts. With regard to stories, however, the matter might be different.

The Value of Stories

Children are typically at home in the world of images. They enjoy stories and can become delightedly engrossed in narratives of all kinds: fairy tales, bedtime stories, biblical stories. Often they will act the stories out in play. If questioned, they can at their respective levels draw appropriate conclusions from stories. Even the youngest can appreciate the practical value of *The Three Little Pigs:* build your house out of solid material. Children can sense that in *Snow White,* as in many fairy tales, good ultimately triumphs over evil. And what child does not understand the moral lesson against lying in *Pinocchio?* This is not to say that they assume such stories are historically factual. On the contrary, they may themselves be the first to assert that they are "just stories."

Assertions of this sort may be less forthcoming with regard to biblical stories since these narratives, even in churches or schools more receptive to critical views of the Bible, are usually told and discussed as a matter of fact without overwhelming the children with critical questions. This procedure appears to be the most appropriate. If the children should ask, however, particularly the older ones, they could be told honestly whether some people feel that some narratives are "just stories," that is, unhistorical. If the answer is that some people do, the teacher or minister might review the differing opinions without denigrating either alternative. Some lessons of a story that can be drawn whether it is "true," or historical, or not could then be made clear. It might be helpful for the teacher or minister to express her or his opinion on the matter along with reasons for the opinion. Equally helpful, perhaps, would be a simple explanation of the preferred interpretive method of the religious community to which the children belong.

The Truth of Stories

Such a response might run like this: "Some people say that this part of the story—that the sun stood still in the sky (Joshua 10:13)—is not true. Whether God did exactly that may not be as important as the fact that God was there to help the Hebrew people in battle; that is what this part of the story teaches. I myself feel that God's power to help in this situation is clearer and more impressive if it really happened that way than if it did not; God made the day longer so that the Hebrews would have time to win."

This approach leaves the children disposed to the persuasion of the minister or teacher but also leaves them free to draw their own conclusions. Whatever they surmise, they will have been prepared for a later time in life when a tolerant hearing of other conclusions might be helpful. If, by parental views or the standards of the religious community, gentle persuasion appears to lack the requisite resoluteness, the teacher or minister may need to adjust accordingly or to deal with the relevant adult parties according to guidelines now to be considered.

Adolescents and Adults

At a certain point, purposely familiarizing adolescent Christians with varying views of biblical interpretation seems quite desirable. The same can be said of adult Christians who have had little exposure to other views. For no matter what the disposition of the congregation, parish, or school in which the ministry or teaching is taking place, most of the members or students will eventually come into contact with views different from their own. The learners, therefore, could profit from exposure to the idea that, no matter which interpretation of the Bible they find the best, there is much to be said for a tolerant respect for other positions.

Part of the procedure suggested here can be used with groups, but with adaptations it is also appropriate for those who may raise the question with a minister or teacher individually. The lesson regarding differing biblical interpretations would probably need to be reinforced regularly. It could be done most naturally by discussing the issues in conjunction with biblical stories and directives whose interpretations are commonly disputed. Pastoral or pedagogical sensitivity to the needs and feelings of those being taught or ministered to would always guide the timing and intensity of these discussions. The procedure resembles that used for children but is more detailed. Not all the points are appropriate for every setting. Discussion, for example, is often not appropriate in situations in which preaching is the primary focus.

1. Present the issues

Here the minister or teacher would lay out the problem in as fair a way as possible. It would be important to show respect for the major positions on the matter. It is difficult for many ministers or teachers at this point to bridle a tendency to sway the listeners in one direction or the other. For the sake of leaving them free for greater tolerance and unanimity, however, blatant demonstration of favoritism should be avoided.

For example: "The infancy narratives of Matthew (1:18–2:23) and Luke (1:5–2:40) are two of the most renowned and beloved parts of the entire Bible. Their warmth and beauty have inspired Christians for centuries. In stimulating and nurturing the annual celebration of Christmas, they have brought spiritual renewal and profound joy to the hearts of Christians everywhere. The spirit of this season has affected entire cultures in which Christians live, so that even non-Christians and nonbelievers are often touched by its wonder.

"According to ancient traditions, Mary was a major source of the story, at least in Luke. She, of course, would have been a reliable witness of the events depicted. The reliability of both Luke and Matthew has been long assumed by most Christians. So the historical nature of the Christmas stories is usually not doubted. Pilgrimages are made to Bethlehem, and scientists continue to theorize about which stellar phenomenon around the early first century would have been called the star that led the wise men to the city of Jesus' birth.

"A good number of modern biblical scholars, however, have noted that many of the details of these stories are theological in nature. This means that the writers consistently use terms or incidents to explain the significance of Jesus, not simply to depict historical details. Since the purpose of history writing among the ancients was more inspirational than scientific, these scholars conclude that the terms or incidents are quite probably literary devices or metaphors—like figures of speech—rather than factual descriptions of what was. The gospel writers wanted to nurture their audience's faith that Jesus appeared in history by the power of the Spirit of God, that Jesus was the long-awaited Messiah, and that he brought God's redeeming presence into the world. For the language and images of their story, they drew more on the Old Testament, or Hebrew Scripture, and on their communities' own inspired insights than on factual memories. Therefore, such scholars say, the historicity or factual nature of much of these narratives is quite suspect.

"On the other hand, from the perspectives of some contemporary interpretive methodologies, it could be argued that, precisely because the narratives are likely designed to be accepted at face value, we do a disservice to both the author and the text by discounting its factual nature. Such an approach to interpretation does not exactly bring us back to historical reliability but does perhaps challenge us to join the early Church—that is, both the scriptural authors and their audiences—in imagining that events occurred as described. This relates to a point to be made momentarily, namely, the spiritual or practical value of the biblical texts."

Once the issues are presented, reactions may be varied, depending on what the listeners' dispositions are and on the focal points of their concerns. Some may feel disturbed, shocked, or even attacked. This is a usual reaction when one's belief system is challenged. It is likely that many of the listeners have absolutized their systems. So the perceived prospect of having to let go of the security that such a system brings can be discomforting. Others may feel defended, supported, or even encouraged in their position. This too is an expected reaction to familiar-sounding opinions. When one hears what is consonant with one's absolutized belief system, faith in that system is frequently reinforced.

If the minister or teacher has presented each of the alternatives in the best light possible, however, there will likely also be some confusion among at least some of the listeners. For if each interpretation has been allowed to sound respectable, the listeners are likely to suspect or perceive some value in the position that is not their own. In other words, those inclined to the fundamentalist position might suspect that there may be something to disputing some of the historicity of the infancy narratives. And those disposed to the critical position might begin to lean toward acknowledging the possible value of accepting such narratives at face value. The belief system of each group would be disturbed. The challenge to the belief system of both kinds of listeners is important in fostering freedom for the kind of tolerance in which the minister or teacher is interested. For an absolutized system of either the fundamentalist or the critical sort makes tolerance quite difficult.

2. Recall some of the primary spiritual aims of such interpretations

In the atmosphere of confusion or challenged systems, the minister can be supportive and nurturing by explaining the spiritual or pastoral implications of the interpretations. Here, the focus would be on what the varying interpretations have in common. This helps the listeners give special attention to those elements of the Christian meaning system that, by the description of the main elements discussed in chapter 2, may be regarded as primary. Such attention can help them eventually become aware, though perhaps not reflexively or consciously, of what may divide them, namely, the apparently secondary element of biblical interpretation in which the questions of historicity and normativeness play an important part.

In other words, the listeners may come to sense that if the story brings believers closer to their Lord and more deeply into faith, the significance of that growth may outweigh the importance of assumptions about whether a story is historically true or a directive is permanently normative. What the minister or teacher would be doing here is helping the listeners to see that the primary elements of their religious awareness are the so-called main elements of the Christian belief system. Where such understanding occurs, the listeners have a greater opportunity to recognize the respectability of alternate systems of biblical interpretation. An example of this step follows:

"Let's look at the stories and react to what they say. Picture Mary in her readiness to be the Savior's mother. Imagine Joseph's confused but obedient response to the angel's announcement. Think of the circumstances that led to the child's being born in the city of David, the city of the Messiah's forebear. Feel the lowliness of the birth in the stable. Sense the awe of the shepherds before the angels who herald this event. Join the shepherds and wise men in homage before this child. With Mary and Joseph open your hearts to love anew this blessing from heaven.

"What faith cannot be touched by such a scene? Inspired words like these have the power to let one sense in an ever deeper, joyful way what it means that the Lord has come into the world, that the Lord is here, humble and obedient, to serve and rescue. Touching persons in this way, the narratives of Matthew and Luke can bring a believer into closer communion with the one of whom the narratives speak. Faith is made more lively through a renewed sense of his presence here, the presence of him who was born into the world. Note that it is through a story that one can respond this way in faith, a story that is *imagined* as a historical event. Some may assume that all of their images are of what truly was; others may assume that certain images are only of what could have been. In either case, the believer is being stimulated through imagination to move toward the Lord of whom the story speaks. In light of this, who are better off, the ones who hold that all details of the stories are factual, or those who contend that certain details are just appropriate inspirational images? I find that question difficult to answer."

3. Weigh the advantages and disadvantages of both interpretations

If at this point the listeners share the minister's or teacher's difficulty in deciding which interpreter is better off, they have probably emotionally or intuitively grasped the implications of pointing to the spiritual or pastoral value of the stories. These implications could, of course, have to do with the minister's or teacher's sense that the questions of historicity or permanent normativeness are of secondary importance.

The awareness of the respect due to both fundamentalist and critical interpretations can be conceptualized or cognitively reinforced by noting some advantages and disadvantages of each. Here, the emphasis is less on the intuitive or emotional and more on the intellectual or cognitive; it is, one could say, more an emphasis on left-brain than on right-brain functions. The listeners are helped to understand what factors weigh for and against each interpretation and thus why a constraining option for one over the other is not necessarily due. The fairness, then, of letting each view freely prevail becomes more apparent. The minister or teacher may express a preference for one of them. But by this time it can be perceived as recommended rather than requisite.

The discussion might proceed like this: "Those who hold for the basic historicity of the narratives are in an enviable position.

Their perspective is often called fundamentalist. The stories for them are intensified in significance by the fact that they are taken as fairly accurate depictions of what actually occurred. These persons then become attuned to the images of the stories in ways that they feel closely parallel the awareness of those who are said to have originally experienced the events of which the stories speak. Such a sense of contact with history is exciting. It brings with it a feeling of closeness to all-important events. It also helps faith remain enthusiastic, believing that God intervenes in history in dramatic, supernatural ways. Many today have lost this kind of enthusiasm.

"But let's not look just at this side of the issue. Many of those who accept critical biblical scholarship are relying on concepts or insights from modern science or academic disciplines that they feel can significantly aid their faith. Though critical interpreters may doubt the historicity of a certain narrative, or at least of some of its details, they can rejoice that the inspired biblical author has added imaginative and interpretive embellishment that helps them appreciate the meaning of the event, no matter how it occurred. This can leave them with a sense of being closer to the Lord than were perhaps some of those who lived through the event historically; for these latter did not have the advantage of an inspired interpreter, namely, a biblical author or editor, to help them deeply grasp in faith what was happening.

"Another advantage of this view is that it allows for solidarity with those who assert that God can use worldly things like science for God's glory and the glory of the Church. Here too, however, there is another side of the story. Those who hold the critical view can be left feeling alienated from the original event, somewhat like outsiders who, excluded from historical experience, are left in a world of images, symbols, and myths that, by comparison, seem less compelling. It can also cause them to wonder whether partial fictiousness undermines the historical credibility of the entire story. This can be a burden to faith or at least deprive it of the awesome awareness that God really intervenes in history through extraordinary means. That is why I personally prefer the first view. I like to think of dramatic demonstrations of God's power. This is inspiring to me, but I can understand how the other view might be more inspiring to someone else."

4. Encourage discussion

At this point, the listeners might be ready to share their feelings or viewpoints, particularly if they feel shocked, confused, or especially supported. A simple question like "What is your first reaction to all of this?" could be enough to trigger their reactions. This sharing will be particularly enriching if there are differing interpretive views in the group. It would also be desirable if both absolutizing and tolerant tendencies were represented. Since people in such groups often seek to be supportive of one another, there is potential to help them develop empathy for—though not necessarily agreement with—positions differing from their own.

The minister or teacher may want to move to a more specific question like "Which interpretation of the infancy narratives do you prefer, the fundamentalist or the critical, and for what reasons?" The likely varying answers to this question should continue to clarify the issues and help offer the possibility of tolerant acceptance of alternate views. This should be the case particularly if the participants have been allowed to share in small groups of about four to seven. Here, the participants will typically feel the least threatened and the most supported.

If time permits, the dispositions being discussed could be sharpened by posing this kind of question: "How might you help calm a dispute in which two people do not agree on which of the two interpretations is better?" Discussion around this question could help the participants become aware of how absolutizing is divisive and how tolerance brings peace. The question may help some participants move in the direction of tolerance. And in teaching others tolerance, they will likely become even more tolerant themselves.

5. Encourage the participants to share their own stories

This step belongs thematically with the discussion just mentioned. Here the question is "What circumstances in your own life have led you to this way of understanding biblical events?" It may have already been discussed in connection with previous questions. As posed explicitly, it best fits perhaps before the final question under step 4. Because of the lengthy and more personal sharing it may stimulate, however, it is dealt with here separately.

Sharing one's personal history as it pertains to the subject of interpretation can help the participants overcome stereotypes about individual faith and individual approaches to the Bible. The minister's own story may be a helpful way to open the discussion. For example: "I was raised a Catholic before the Second Vatican Council. My parents taught me to love and rely on the Lord but did not mention the Bible very much. Even in the parish school, our formation focused more on the sacraments and on Catholic doctrine than on Scripture. It wasn't until college and the seminary that I was exposed to the Bible in depth. This was a wonderful experience for me. An exciting and inspiring world opened up. The context, however, was that of critical biblical interpretation, the kind of scholarship we have been talking about. This impressed me. Therefore, it is very difficult for me to talk about issues of historicity or norma–tiveness without thinking about such scholarly opinions.

"I, therefore, tend to share the opinion that much of the infancy narratives is not historical. On the other hand, when I pray with the Bible or celebrate feasts such as Christmas, such matters usually concern me very little, if at all. I just try to open myself to the words of the text or to the events described, to enter into the story with my imagination, and to let the Spirit touch me and lead me. At such moments it is *as if* all of the events of the biblical stories are historically factual."

6. Employ nonpartisan language

This is not an additional step in the process. It is, rather, a ministerial or pedagogical technique that can demonstrate general respect for the differing views of biblical interpretation. As such, it is a technique that one can employ more when the issue of interpretation is not explicitly under discussion. It consists of phraseology that avoids implying that the minister or teacher is a partisan to or an advocate of one position over the other. It thus can model the kind of tolerance for which the minister or teacher wants to leave the hearers free. To those who are sensitive to the issues, it could also show that the minister or teacher has adopted a position of second naiveté as described in this book, namely with respect to one's interpretive methodology and to the biblical texts themselves.

For example, the minister could say, "A star led the wise men to Jesus," "The writer probably invented the star that he says led the wise men to Jesus," or "The writer says a star led the wise men to Jesus." The differences among the three statements are small but could be quite significant. The first statement says there was a star and suggests that this claim is historically factual; the first statement could thus be taken as supportive of a fundamentalist interpretation. The second statement suggests that the star is a literary device and thus not historically factual; the second statement could thus be taken as supportive of a critical interpretation. So either statement could reinforce the absolutizing of the position that each statement appears to support. The third statement, however, merely observes that in the Gospel of Matthew a star is mentioned and leaves room for either a fundamentalist or critical interpretation; the third statement then could be taken as supportive of a tolerant disposition toward either interpretation.

The technique simply involves mentioning the source and the statements drawn from it without interpreting them as to literalness. One might also say something like "According to the story, a star led the wise men to Jesus." This technique, already quite widespread in teaching and preaching, is sometimes used to avoid alienating different listeners or to avoid dealing with the issue altogether. Here, it could play the positive role of leaving individuals free to maintain their respective positions, to recognize the value of another position, or to assume—at least implicitly—a position of second naiveté.

Academic Settings

Reflection and Study

In colleges, universities, and seminaries, the issues can be studied at higher levels of reflection, the implications can be pondered more leisurely, and the modeling of tolerance can influence many present and future leaders. Such things can be done both in classes and through campus ministry or formation programs. Not only Scripture courses but also courses in such areas as world religions, philosophy of religion, and foundational theology are appropriate arenas. Chapel exercises, retreats, and other spiritual activities are likewise appropriate. Therefore, the possibilities discussed above regarding adolescents and adults apply here at a level of intensity or reflection accommodated to the situation. Not all the points discussed would necessarily be suitable. Some professors, for example, might not feel that personal sharing is always appropriate in academic discussions. Conversely, some points can be considered here that do not seem to be appropriate for general adolescent and adult groups.

A systematic study of the nature of faith and its relationship to biblical revelation could be very helpful in sensitizing students to the possible value of greater tolerance for varying interpretations of biblical texts. Such study may also give rise to assessing the value of second naiveté or similar dispositions regarding biblical stories or regarding one's method of biblical interpretation. A systems approach is one method of laying out many of the issues and reflecting on their implications. Other methods that could be used along with or in place of system theory include hermeneutics, language philosophy, sociology of knowledge, sociology of religion, and psychology of religion.

The students' experience with teachers and other campus leaders whose interpretations of the Bible lean clearly to either the fundamentalist or critical viewpoints could facilitate this study. Since modeling is such a powerful teaching tool, such leaders might best be those who likewise exhibit tolerance or recognition of alternate positions.

Helping students in ways like these to accept their own tendencies to absolutize their belief systems could lead them to a heightened awareness of the risks of absolutizing. Such awareness seems to be important for the salutary effects of religion on the world and for the fruitful mission of the Church. Knowing where the problems lie is often the first step toward their solution. Thus it may also be helpful to discuss priorities and attempt to judge with students to what extent the absolutizing that separates religious persons and religious groups is worth the price of possible diminished spiritual growth and effectiveness. Is the Church being victimized by narrow visions of how the biblical word binds it? How valuable might mutual recognition be? How valuable is something like second naiveté? The answers of students, faculty, and campus ministers to questions like these appear to depend on the extent to which they value—and even want to foster—appropriate diversity in expressions of Christian faith.

Institutional Approaches

Some institutions might want to take purposeful steps to foster an ecumenical or tolerant approach to the matter of biblical interpretation. They could encourage a balanced and scholarly discussion of biblical interpretations in designated classes; such interpretations could be representative of a broad range of faith dispositions. Institutions could also commit themselves to balanced representation in the appointment of faculty members and in the selection of speakers for chapel services and other functions. Caricaturing or even intimidating persons because of their particular theologies or methods of biblical interpretation could be regarded as unprofessional or even unethical. Initiatives such as these could add depth and strength to students' personal persuasions and to the variety of methodologies whereby Christianity attempts to carry out the mission to which it believes it is called. Though not a facile solution to a complex problem, steps like these could exemplify how the matter of biblical interpretation can appear as a controverted issue that need not deter the Church from deepened spirituality and a unified dedication to Christianity's goals. Academe's scientific and scholarly treatment of varying biblical interpretations could thus demonstrate both tolerance and respectability.

Summary

The work of the Church requires ministry to believers according to their specific needs. Therefore, respect for varying interpretations of the Bible would appear to be a primary characteristic of those ministers or teachers who nurture others through expounding the Bible. Nonetheless, there are appropriate times for caring confrontation regarding individuals' specific approaches to the scriptural texts. The goal of such confrontation would be to nurture a freedom for the recognition of an alternate manner of biblical interpretation. Fostered in an atmosphere of mutual respect and support, such recognition could lead to deepened spirituality and more effective work of the Church.

Children, especially the younger ones, probably should seldom be exposed to such issues. At their request, however, the matter could be discussed frankly and in simple terms. Alternate views would be presented; a spiritual message common to both views would be stressed as the primary purpose of the text; and the children would feel free to choose either view, though the minister's or teacher's appropriate expression of a preference could be desirable.

Adolescents and adults would be exposed to the issues at appropriate times. The minister or teacher would present the issues, emphasize the primary message of a given text, weigh the advantages and disadvantages of each interpretation, encourage discussion, and—having employed nonpartisan language throughout the process—encourage the sharing of the group members' own stories.

In institutions of higher learning, both in and outside the classroom, the approach would resemble that for adults generally but would be more intense and reflective. It might also include discussion of system theory or any other frame of reference for understanding the risks of absolutizing and the possible desirability of mutual recognition between two cultures of belief.

Chapter 6

The Love
of Mystery

Beyond the Biblical Debate

Agreement on Essentials

W ithin a systems perspective, the fundamentalist approach can be treated as a method of biblical inter-pretation characterized by a tendency to absolutize a specific Christian system in which the events depicted or norms proclaimed are understood to be primarily factual or permanently binding and to be calling for a mostly literal interpretation. In a parallel way, the critical approach to the Bible can be treated as a method of interpretation characterized by a tendency to absolutize a specific Christian system in which the biblical events depicted or norms proclaimed are understood to be more or less factual or binding, depending on a number of factors affecting the design and use of the text, but especially on the specific literary form through which each event or norm is recounted, and thus to be calling for a larger variety of interpretations.

A way to unity, though not necessarily uniformity, might open when advocates of both cultures of belief acknowledge that acceptable distinctions could be made between what is primary and what is secondary in their respective systems. In professing commitment to what is primary, namely, the general growth and work of Christianity as characterized by the "five main elements," and in asserting that varying methods of biblical interpretation are secondary, they would be recognizing the value of one another's positions and even promoting them in sensitive and positive ways. Undesirable and variable elements in one another's systems would be critically distinguished from those elements inherent to the definition of each system.

The fundamentalist and critical approaches so described and debated could thus give way to approaches that reap far more the advantages of tolerance and run far less the risks of absolutizing. They could give way to visions of biblical interpretation that foster more peace than conflict in the Church and academe and thus also foster new visions of the Church itself. In this sense, a systems approach to exegetical rivalry would not only delineate anew two major systems in conflict but could lead as well to systems of peace. Here, Christians of varying cultures of belief could avoid the fallacy of Christian certitude, minister to one another, and bring their many common values to bear more effectively and persuasively on culture and society (Neuhaus, 246–47, 260, 264).

Familiar Words in a Fresh Context

If such harmony were to ensue, one might well wonder if these approaches would best be called fundamentalist and critical anymore. Various neologisms might come under consideration: *neofundamentalism; neocriticalism; tolerant fundamentalism; post-critical biblical criticism*; or even, in light of the second naiveté that would characterize them, such unconventional designations as *critical fundamentalism* and *fundamentalist biblical criticism*. Titles like these might have an immediate advantage of facilitating communication among those who might resonate with or share a systems approach or some other arbitrating approach to the issues.

One might wonder, however, if in the long run names of this sort would not contribute to the very separation and faction-building they were designed to help diminish. Would "neofunda–mentalists" or "neocriticalists" want to raise their banners and thus risk the pitfalls of "neoabsolutism" or "post-tolerance intolerance"? For as the systems approach taken in this book suggests, in any system—even in a systems-analyzing system—there is danger of forgetting an important principle, namely, that an alternate system can in theory represent what is objectively right or best. Neologisms could thus risk fueling absolutism on either side and thus risk undermining the success and sincerity of the tolerance and recognition that appear to be desirable.

Beyond this, though, language functions well with many words whose meanings are quite relative to circumstances; *faith, love, freedom,* and *duty* are clear examples. The faith of a child or neophyte may be quite real but quite different from, though analogous to, the faith of an adult or a believer of long commitment; love to an agnostic may be quite different from, though in many ways similar to, love to a mystic. Words and nomenclature then have a fluidity to which context gives specificity.

It would seem appropriate, then, to speak plainly of fundamentalist and critical approaches to the Bible and to leave it to the context to clarify whether such interpretations are functioning as elements of tolerant or intolerant systems. The context would specify to what degree a system in question is tolerant or intolerant. Figure C shows fundamentalist and critical approaches at different places on a scale from complete intolerance (0) to complete tolerance (100). In this example, the fundamentalist disposition might be called somewhat tolerant and the critical disposition rather intolerant. The positions can vary widely on the scale, however, depending on whose fundamentalist or whose critical disposition is under discussion.

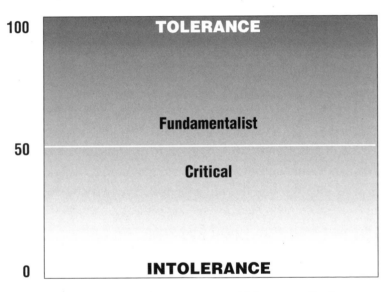

Figure C. Dispositions on a Tolerance Scale

Nonbiblical Contexts of the Debate

Such fluidity also appears to be desirable in another way. The discussion of exegetical rivalry in the previous chapters focused mainly on the question of historicity relating to biblical stories—such as those of Genesis, Jonah, or the gospels—and to biblical norms like commandments and exhortations. It is in these terms that the discussion is most commonly understood. Nonetheless, one can point to other kinds of fundamentalist approaches and other kinds of critical interpretations that occasion rivalry and division in the worldwide Christian religion. Such divisions, occurring both within and between denominations, are multiple. When Church leadership is exercised assertively or obeyed with unquestioning deference, for example, one might well speak of a certain fundamentalism regarding authority. Where authoritative directives are given or responded to with various degrees of sensitivity to their perceived appropriateness, one might rightly regard the disposition as a critical one.

A similar comparison is possible regarding the doctrines that have in various ecclesial communities come from Church authorities or traditions. The kind of dogmatics that assumes that the immediate and literal understanding of doctrinal tenets is the only possible interpretation could be regarded as fundamentalist. An interpretation of doctrines that seeks to elucidate them in light of historical circumstances could fairly be named critical. Elucidations of sacramental elements (such as the substance of Eucharistic bread or the permanency of marriage) that are rooted in traditional perceptions of nonambiguousness can often appear quite fundamentalist in character. Where such elements are interpreted in light of other factors—say, piety or the complexity of human actions—a critical disposition might be seen at work. Some ethical or disciplinary norms are not expressly articulated in the Bible. When such directives are regarded inflexibly as binding in all situations, the disposition could fittingly be regarded as fundamentalist. Where moral directives are applied in light of specific circumstances and individual consciences, something more like a critical view of the matter might well be involved.

Examples such as these show that with respect to fundamentalist and critical approaches to issues in the Church, the arenas of tolerance and recognition are numerous. Figure D shows four areas to which, besides the Bible, these basic interpretive stances can be applied: authority, doctrine, sacramentality, and morality. Those fundamentalist dispositions in areas graphed toward the bottom (0) of the scale could be called rather intolerant. Those critical dispositions in areas located toward the top (100) of the scale could be called somewhat tolerant. There is no necessary correlation between areas in which the two basic dispositions can operate. In other words, some individuals, communities, or denominations might be more or less fundamentalist in some areas and more or less critical in others; and there seems to be no rule by which the extent of tolerance or intolerance in one area relates to the degree of tolerance or intolerance in another area.

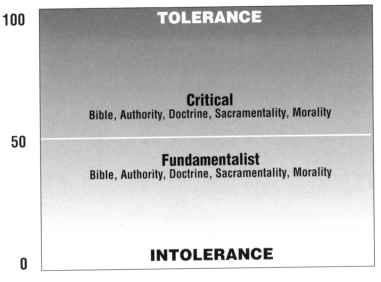

Figure D. Dispositions and Areas
on a Tolerance Scale

Thus, for example, an individual or community might be quite intolerantly fundamentalist regarding ecclesiastical authority and rather tolerantly critical regarding social morality. This variability of tolerance between areas of fundamentalist or critical interpretation is probably more the rule than the exception. Within the systems approach being explored here, however, the location of the area (that is, as fundamentalist or critical) would appear to be insignificant. What is suggested as ideal is that individuals, communities, and denominations—indeed the entire Church—be 100 percent tolerant in all areas, whether the fundamentalist or the critical prevails, as long as in each case the main elements of the general Christian system are apparent, and as long as issues regarding any apparently undesirable but variable elements have been appropriately discussed and, at least through acceptable compromise, resolved. An ideal like this presumes that such tolerance—and the seemingly desirable recognition that could ensue—springs from interpretive systems that can coexist in harmony and mutual assistance.

A consideration of areas of interpretation other than the one related to the historicity or normativeness of biblical texts shows how, in a systems approach, a variety of religious issues not often associated with exegetical rivalry can be seen as related to it. A likely reason that such an association is not always made is that other kinds of issues—for example, developmental, societal, and political—seem to impinge on these religious areas with greater force than the biblical issues. This holds even though one could show that the issues involved in all the areas are somehow related to biblical texts. For example, stances regarding abortion often appear to have more to do with personal sensitivity and societal influence than with biblical injunctions against killing that might be interpreted in either fundamentalist or critical ways.

Nonreligious Contexts of Analogous Debates

Yet perhaps the personal or social values involved in such stances are themselves being interpreted in either fundamentalist or critical ways. With this in mind, a systems approach can be taken well beyond the matter of exegetical rivalry and even beyond religious debate. To consider in detail all or even some of these kinds of issues is beyond the scope of this book. It seems appropriate, however, to mention a few additional issues as an incentive to further discussion of them in terms of system theory.

These are areas that are part of the secular arena but that clearly have implications for the Church and are influenced by the Church. The areas of cultural diversity, feminism, economic systems, and international relations are examples. In each area, one could point to fundamentalist and critical constituencies and also make a case for the value of mutual tolerance or recognition.

Cultural Tension

Racial or ethnic strife could be seen as a result of absolutizing a meaning system in which the race or heritage of persons in a given culture is regarded as a main element or the primary source of discord. To the extent that the perceived superiority of a given race or ethnic group is taken literally, the disposition could be called fundamentalist. The agents of such absolutizing could be exhorted to seek a harmony that would come from an acceptance of the secondary nature of race or ethnicity in cultural systems, especially "multicultural" ones. In a parallel way, the opposing faction, understood as critical, might be exhorted to work for a more efficient type of "integration" or "multiculturalism" that could result if the critical faction's own disposition were approached with second naiveté. Here, the main values of equality and justice might best be served because tolerance, acceptance, and respect have led to both racial or ethnic pride *and* racial or ethnic indifference that, combined in a new order, are no longer destructive but edifying, and not just for favorites of the "politically correct."

Gender Issues

The liberation of women—and thus of the male populace with whom women are inexorably bound in social and cultural systems—might be viewed as ending the absolutizing of assumptions connected with gender. This could be seen to apply as much to fundamentalist men and women who are intolerant of nontraditional sex roles as to critical men and women who are intolerant of traditional sex roles. As long as the elimination of exploitation and abuse of all persons—including children of both genders—is viewed as primary, the matter of gender-related roles, viewed traditionally or nontraditionally, could remain secondary. By such a scheme, there might be room for a new harmonization of traditional and nontraditional values regarding both men and women. For example, people might learn to accept that patriarchy, as neither absolutely normative nor inherently evil, can help provide nest and nurture to the young, as long as no one in the family or social system is being exploited.

Economic and Social Structures

The same could be argued with respect to competing economic systems in which fairness, the interest of all concerned, and the dignity of the human person are accepted as the primary values. In such a perspective, the merits of socialist and capitalist systems, or of "Western" and "non-Western" ideologies, even though interpreted in a fundamentalist way, might be much more apparent. And second naiveté toward the dispositions that in original naiveté make capitalists and socialists, or Westerners and non-Westerners, one another's determined critics might lead to greater creativity in seeking solutions to problems in which both are interested. Here, it might become apparent that the abuses to which parties on both sides might rightfully point in one another's systems spring more from the bilateral absolutizing of the systems than from the systems themselves.

In such a perspective, there could be a revitalization of international relations. Fears that lead to competition, defense, deterrence, terrorism, and warfare of various temperatures because of absolutized ideologies might cease to be the victor over a humanizing naiveté regarding the "opposition's" potential for attaining humanitarian objectives. For example, the events in eastern Europe and Soviet Asia that led to and followed upon the collapse of the Berlin Wall in 1989 need not be taken as evidence of communism's inherent wrongness or of capitalism's inherent rightness. Revolution, whether by bullet or ballot, can merely signify the need to alter variable elements in a political or social system that has much in its favor. Here and in other circumstances, even where religious differences prevail, self-righteousness on either side regarding the "opposition" in its essential features can be part of a process of self-defeat.

Christianity and Other Religions

Christianity's Respect and Tolerance

Another specific example of the application of system theory to arenas of human questioning and struggle involves the significance of Christianity among many other religions of the world. In previous chapters, various differentiated systems of Christianity were viewed as alternate systems within the general Christian system. The main elements of this system were presented as Jesus Christ, his Cross, his Resurrection, the Bible, and the Church.

Christianity, then, in its various forms, was seen as a distinctive form of religiousness.

Religiousness was depicted as a part of a general system in which feelings, activities, objects, social structures, and images and concepts all correlate with synthesizing systems to impinge on and be influenced by faith or religiousness vis-à-vis other such forms, that is, vis-à-vis other religions.

In terms of fundamentalist and critical approaches to the Bible, it was noted that there are risks in absolutizing specific elaborated Christian systems and apparent advantages to recognizing the value of alternate systems within Christianity.

At this point, then, it might seem possible to draw a parallel between the absolutizing of a differentiated Christian system and the absolutizing of Christianity (or the general Christian system) as such. For even as the tolerance of alternate Christian systems would involve admitting the possibility of their truth or superiority—and this without sacrificing commitment to one's own differentiated Christian system—the stance of Christianity vis-à-vis other religions could appear to be open to a similar sort of tolerance. In this perspective, Christianity would be lived as a satisfying form of religiousness, and Christians would also recognize the value of other religions without making any absolute judgments regarding their objective value.

As noted earlier, such a stance is typical of Eastern religions. It can be also found in liberal theologies of Western religions such as liberal Protestantism, Reform Judaism, and Islamic Sufism. Dispositions like these could seemingly do much to bring greater harmony to the dialogue between religions and even contribute to peace in a world torn by strife often rooted in or fomented by religious intolerance.

Traditionally interpreted doctrines of Christianity, however, do not permit such dispositions. Here, the truth of God's supreme saving act in Jesus Christ's Cross and Resurrection is proclaimed as the objective norm of all religiousness. More succinctly, Jesus Christ is believed to be either the supreme way, or, for some, the only way to salvation (see John 14:67). This does not necessarily amount to a denial of other religions' value. In fact, most Christians regard them as valuable, even greatly valuable, for numerous reasons but especially because they seem somehow to relate to God's saving will as expressed through Jesus Christ. There are many theologies of this relationship, such as those that see the value of non-Christian faith as somehow dependent on an implicit or hidden connection with Christ's salvific mission for the whole world. Thus good and fruitful dialogue goes on between Christianity and other religions. In many cases, Christians are learning much from the insights and practices of others. Christians thus accord other religions a certain kind of deep and sincere recognition.

Christianity's Absolute Certainty About Itself

Traditional teachings, however, prohibit many Christians from according to others the kind of unconditional recognition that others can accord to them. Through a systems approach to the issues, such a prohibition may be perceived as merely part of absolutizing, where the absolute mediated by the system is identified as inseparable from the system. Here, the mediation would be taken to be as absolute as the God who is mediated. In other words, through a systems approach it could be argued that the permanent and unequaled link between God and the main elements of *Christian* systems is itself perceived in traditional Christian faith as a matter of primary importance. Therefore, for such faith, a designation of this link as secondary, in comparison with the elements of another more encompassing religious system, is not possible. And this is often the case for both fundamentalist and critical Christians. At issue here is the possibility of perceiving the specifically Christian expression of religiousness as secondary to a more encompassing system of religiousness itself. But with an admission of this possibility might appear to come a relativizing of Christianity among the world's great religions.

Within the perspectives and perceptions of this book there does not seem to be evidence for arguing any further than that such a possibility exists. Saying that the *possibility* exists, however, is not the same as saying that it is the case. In Christian terms, in other words, it means that if God so willed it, redemption through faith in the crucified and risen Jesus Christ could be one authentic path of salvific religiousness among many. Asserting, then, what God could possibly do need not deny what God has done or may have done. What, in fact, individual Christians and Christian communities profess within their respective religious systems is another matter. And when their professions of faith include claims to Christianity's supremacy among religions, it can also be argued that here, faith's absolutizing may well indeed conform with what is so, even if one does not succumb to the fallacy of Christian certitude, even if the full truth of the so-called objective situation is not accessible to the believer except in conjunction with religious faith. Even if "naive" faith in the literalness of the Bible's multiple expressions of Christianity's exclusivity or supremacy among religions should give way to second naiveté regarding such texts, the situation need not necessarily be any different. For responding to a text *as if* it is so is not necessarily to deny *that* it is so.

Thus from the systems perspective offered here, where even absolute certainty regarding what is ultimately so appears to be necessarily conjoined with some kind of faith, one can competently assert and persuasively defend Christianity's superiority or not. In either case, though, one could be better disposed to avoid the dangers of absolutizing and to be gainfully affected by tolerance. It may appear, then, as profitable to suggest that those on both sides of the issue ask whether one or the other side better serves the purpose in which both contingents appear to be interested ultimately, namely, the purpose of facilitating authentic religiousness and the various desirable transformations that ensue from religion.

In other words, certain questions appear to be in order for anyone, Christian or not, on whom the absolutizing tendency of religiousness has had an influence. Does one disposition toward absolutizing nurture faith more than another? If one of them does, why? And even if one of them does, what can be said of tolerating and recognizing the other? Such questions seem to be crucial for this debate and thus for all those who through tolerance and recognition may want, in a world too torn by strife, to turn systems of conflict into systems of peace.

Mystery and Beyond

Firmness of Faith

Tolerance can be a way of saying in a systems perspective that ultimate meaning is elusive (McKnight, 60). Faith that has learned the lesson of tolerance can be a faith that is conscious of its own weakness. This weakness need not be a languor or infirmity but a susceptibility and fragility. It is faith whose weakness for the divine can leave it receptive to the strength that may come only from the divine. Faith like this is firm only in that it knows where it stands. And it does not claim to stand on its own but in holy power and by the grace that it senses to be from heaven. A Christian faith that does not trust itself or its own belief system as much as it trusts its Lord might be able to trust that its Lord empowers faith in a variety of ways, even ways that may appear in human terms to be weak.

The Strength of Love

This is the weakness and strength of faith that—fundamentalist or critical—might be able to recognize the weakness and strength of faith that is different, even when that other faith appears radically different, even if that other faith absolutizes its own belief system or absolutizes a determination not to absolutize anything. For a faith that distrusts its own strengths may realize that all true faith has been caught by the allure of a mystery that is ultimately unspeakable. Such faith may realize that the mystery is such that it overflows as divine transforming goodness while it draws back and calls faith to ever greater heights and depths. Such faith realizes that there is a risk in allowing itself to be so allured, the risk of feeling weak and unsure, and the risk of making mistakes in the process.

But in its weakness such faith knows that there is no more reasonable and exhilarating risk. For the faith of some, this is the risk of love, the risk of having what is most important for having given up what one may have regarded as essential for oneself. Faith that lives like this is a faith that loves the mystery by which faith endures. The love of mystery for such faith is a love that may know but one certain truth, that it loves and is loved in what may at times appear as darkness in the midst of eternal light. A crucial question thus remains: "Amid the plurality of belief systems, who knows where this light shines best?"

Summary

Fundamentalist and critical interpreters of the Bible would seem to profit greatly from avoiding the fallacy of Christian certitude while guarding against any absolutizing that unnecessarily disturbs the harmony by which Christians might live and work together. This cautiousness would pertain not only to the fundamentalist and critical systems of biblical interpretation, to the two cultures of belief that are characterized by rivalry as discussed in this book. The caution would appear as well to be advisable in other matters in which so-called fundamentalist and critical religious dispositions may be involved. Matters like these that belong to such areas as Church authority, doctrine, sacramentality, and morality. Insights here may even be applied to the secular areas of cultural identity, feminism, economics, and international relations. The tolerance that could result from a systemic and ecumenical approach to differences appears, then, to belong to the fabric of faith itself, even in a special way for Christian faith that distinguishes itself from other religions. For faith appears as a continued response to what is believed to be the holy or God, a response in which the greatest certainty may be no more than the certainty of divine mystery, a mystery known to many as love.

Definitions

Absolutizing: concluding that one's meaning system is the normative one or the best one.

Critical: characterized by a preference for fewer literal interpretations of texts or statements because of a conclusion that many different literary forms serve to communicate truths through narratives that appear as factual or permanently normative.

Differentiated System: a variant of a general system in that certain elements distinguish it but not enough to constitute an entirely unique general system.

Faith: a form of well-being in which a person, despite obstacles and mystery, enjoys what is sensed as a satisfying relationship with the divine.

Fundamentalist: characterized by a preference for mostly literal interpretations of texts or statements because of a conclusion that objective reporting is the primary literary form serving to communicate truths through narratives that appear as factual or permanently normative.

General Religious System: a broad and complex but organic and mutually conditioning coalescence of religious elements.

General System: a broad and complex but organic and mutually conditioning coalescence of elements.

Mediation: a means by which a reality is conveyed or communicated.

Meaning System: see *General System.*

Religiousness: see *Faith.*

Second Naiveté: a critical or interpretive disposition whereby one responds to or understands a symbol, mediation, text, or interpretive system without fully relinquishing an awareness of that same symbol, mediation, text, or interpretive system responded to originally through uncritical or unassuming naiveté.

Subsystem: a less inclusive organic and mutually conditioning coalescence of elements that in themselves form another element within a more inclusive or general system.

Synthesizing System: an attitude, conceptual construct, or mental framework by which one experiences a system as organized and coherent.

System Theory: a science aimed at understanding the organized and organic structure of reality or life at all levels.

Variable Elements: elements within a system that are not essential to a definition of the system as a specific one.

Works Cited

Ammerman, Nancy Tatom. *Bible Believers: Fundamentalists in the Modern World.* New Brunswick, N.J.: Rutgers, 1987.

Ashcraft, Morris, "The Strengths and Weaknesses of Fundamentalism," in *The Proceedings of the Conference on Biblical Inerrancy 1987* (Nashville: Broadman, 1987) 531–41.

Averill, Lloyd J. *Religious Right, Religious Wrong.* New York: Pilgrim, 1989.

Barr, James. *Fundamentalism.* Philadelphia: Westminster, 1978.

———. *The Scope and Authority of the Bible.* Philadelphia: Westminster, 1980.

Bertalanffy, Ludwig von. *General System Theory.* New York: Braziller, 1968.

Boone, Kathleen C. *The Bible Tells Them So: The Discourse of Protestant Fundamentalism*. Albany, N.Y.: State University of New York Press, 1989.

Bowker, John W., "Information Process, Systems Behavior, and the Study of Religion," *Zygon* 11 (1976): 361–79.

Branick, Vincent P. "The Attractiveness of Fundamentalism." In *Fundamentalism Today: What Makes It So Attractive?* ed. Marla J. Selvidge. Elgin, Ill.: Brethren, 1984.

Corey, Gerald. *Theory and Practice of Group Counseling*. Monterey, Calif.: Brooks/Cole, 1985.

Davidson, Mark. *Uncommon Sense: The Life and Thought of Ludwig von Bertalanffy (1901–1972), Father of General Systems Theory*. Los Angeles: Tarcher, 1983.

Dillon, John A., Jr. *Foundation of General Systems Theory*. Seaside, Calif.: Intersystems Publications, 1983.

Ellis, E. Earle, "Historical-Literary Criticism—after Two Hundred Years: Origins, Aberrations, Contributions, Limitations," in *The Proceedings of the Conference on Biblical Inerrancy 1987* (Nashville: Broadman, 1987) 411–21.

Elton, G. R. *The Practice of History*. New York: Crowell, 1967.

Evans, Rod L., and Irwin M. Berent. *Fundamentalism: Hazards and Heartbreaks*. La Salle, Ill.: Open Court, 1988.

Falwell, Jerry, ed., with Ed Dobson and Ed Hindson. *The Fundamentalist Phenomenon.* Garden City, N.Y.: Doubleday, 1981.

Fowler, James W. *Stages of Faith: The Psychology of Human Development and the Quest for Meaning.* San Francisco: Harper, 1981.

Fowler, Jim, and Sam Keen. *Life Maps: Conversations on the Journey of Faith.* Waco, Tex.: Word, 1978.

Groome, Thomas H. *Christian Religious Education: Sharing Our Story and Vision.* San Francisco: Harper, 1980.

Heidegger, Martin. *The Question of Being.* Trans. William Kluback and Jean T. Wilde. London: Vision, 1968.

Inbody, Tyron Lee. "What Liberals and Fundamentalists Have in Common." In *Fundamentalism Today: What Makes It So Attractive?* ed. Marla J. Selvidge. Elgin, Ill.: Brethren, 1984.

Johnson, Christopher. *System and Writing in the Philosophy of Jacques Derrida.* Cambridge: Cambridge University Press, 1993.

Jung, C. G. *Memories, Dreams, Reflections.* Ed. Aniela Jaffé. Trans. Richard and Clara Winston. New York: Random House, 1965.

———. *The Undiscovered Self.* Trans. R. F. C. Hull. New York: New American Library, 1958.

Keegan, Terence J. *Interpreting the Bible: A Popular Introduction to Biblical Hermeneutics.* Mahwah, N.J.: Paulist, 1985.

Kitson Clark, G. S. R. *The Critical Historian.* New York: Basic, 1967.

Klemm, David E. *The Hermeneutical Theory of Paul Ricoeur.* Lewisburg, Pa.: Bucknell University Press, 1983.

Krentz, Edgar. *The Historical-Critical Method.* Philadelphia: Fortress, 1975.

Laszlo, Ervin. *Introduction to Systems Philosophy: Toward a New Paradigm of Contemporary Thought.* New York: Gordon and Breach, 1972.

Lines, Timothy Arthur. *Systemic Religious Education.* Birmingham, Ala.: Religious Education Press, 1987.

McKnight, Edgar V. *Postmodern Use of the Bible: The Emergence of Reader-Oriented Criticism.* Nashville: Abingdon, 1988.

Marsden, George M. *Fundamentalism and American Culture: The Shaping of Twentieth-century Evangelicalism: 1870–1925.* New York: Oxford University Press, 1980.

———. *Reforming Fundamentalism. Fuller Seminary and the New Evangelicalism.* Grand Rapids, Mich.: Eerdmans, 1987.

Marty, Martin E., and R. Scott Appleby. *The Glory and the Power: The Fundamentalist Challenge to the Modern World.* Boston: Beacon, 1992.

———. "A Sacred Cosmos, Scandalous Code, Defiant Society." In *Fundamentalisms and Society: Reclaiming the Sciences, the Family, and Education.* ed. Martin E. Marty and Scott Appleby. Vol.

2 of *The Fundamentalism Project* (3 vols.). Chicago: University of Chicago Press, 1993.

Mendelsohn, Everett. "Religious Fundamentalism and the Sciences." In *Fundamentalisms and Society: Reclaiming the Sciences, the Family, and Education.* ed. Martin E. Marty and Scott Appleby. Vol. 2 of *The Fundamentalism Project* (3 vols.). Chicago: University of Chicago Press, 1993.

Miller, James Grier. *Living Systems.* New York: McGraw-Hill, 1978.

Morgan, Robert, and John Barton. *Biblical Interpretation.* Oxford: Oxford University Press, 1988.

Neuhaus, Richard John. *The Naked Public Square.* Grand Rapids, Mich.: Eerdmans, 1984.

Nielsen, Niels C., Jr. *Fundamentalism, Mythos, and World Religions.* Albany, N.Y.: State University of New York Press, 1993.

Noll, Mark A. *Between Faith and Criticism: Evangelicals, Scholarship, and the Bible in America.* San Francisco: Harper, 1986.

O'Collins, Gerald. *Interpreting Jesus.* Mahwah, N.J.: Paulist, 1983.

O'Connell, Colin, "A Heideggerian Analysis of Fundamentalism: A Brief Discussion," *Journal of Dharma* 15 (1990): 114–24.

Peters, Ted, "Sola Scriptura and the Second Naiveté," *Dialog* 16 (1977): 268–80.

Poland, Lynn M. *Literary Criticism and Biblical Hermeneutics: A Critique of Formalist Approaches*. Chico, Calif.: Scholars Press, 1985.

Ricoeur, Paul. *The Conflict of Interpretations: Essays in Hermeneutics.* Ed. Don Ihde. Evanston, Ill.: Northwestern University Press, 1974.

––––––. *The Symbolism of Evil.* Trans. Emerson Buchanan. Boston: Beacon, 1969.

––––––. *Time and Narrative,* 3 vols. Trans. Kathleen McLaughlin and David Pellauer. Chicago: University of Chicago Press, 1984.

Russell, C. Allyn. *Voices of American Fundamentalism.* Philadelphia: Westminster, 1976.

Smith, Page. *The Historian and History.* New York: Vintage, 1964.

Soulen, Richard N. *Handbook of Biblical Criticism.* 2d ed. Atlanta: John Knox, 1981.

Spong, John Shelby. *Rescuing the Bible from Fundamentalism: A Bishop Rethinks the Meaning of Scripture.* San Francisco: Harper, 1991.

Springer, Sally P., and George Deutsch. *Left Brain, Right Brain.* 4th ed. San Francisco: Freeman, 1993.

Stanford, Michael. *The Nature of Historical Knowledge.* Oxford: Basil Blackwell, 1986.

Tate, W. Randolph. *Biblical Interpretation: An Integrated Approach.* Peabody, Mass.: Hendrickson, 1991.

Tilley, Terrence W. "Reformed Epistemology and Religious Fundamentalism: How Basic Are Our Basic Beliefs?" *Modern Theology* 6 (1990): 237–57.

Towne, Edgar A. "Fundamentalism's Theological Challenge to the Churches." In *Fundamentalism Today: What Makes It So Attractive?* ed. Marla J. Selvidge. Elgin, Ill.: Brethren, 1984.

Tracy, David. *Plurality and Ambiguity: Hermeneutics, Religion, Hope.* San Francisco: Harper, 1987.

Trevor-Roper, H. R. *History and Imagination.* Oxford: Clarendon, 1980.

Vanhoozer, Kevin J. *Biblical Narrative in the Philosophy of Paul Ricoeur: A Study in Hermeneutics and Theology.* Cambridge: Cambridge University Press, 1990.

Van Seters, John. *In Search of History: Historiography in the Ancient World and the Origins of Biblical History.* New Haven, Conn.: Yale, 1983.

Wallace, Mark L. *The Second Naiveté: Barth, Ricoeur, and the New Yale Theology.* Macon, Ga.: Mercer University Press, 1990.

Wink, Walter. *The Bible in Human Transformation: Toward a New Paradigm for Biblical Study.* Philadelphia: Fortress, 1973.

————. *Transforming Bible Study: A Leader's Guide.* Nashville: Abingdon, 1980.

Wittgenstein, Ludwig. *On Certainty.* Ed. G.E.M. Anscombe and G. H. von Wright. Trans. Denis Paul and G.E.M. Anscombe. New York: Harper, 1972.

Index

Subjects and Names

Scriptural References

About
the Author

Ronald Quillo was raised in St. Louis, Missouri, and there attended Cardinal Glennon College. Interest in other cultures led him to France and Germany, where he earned graduate degrees. His doctorate in theology, acquired in 1977, is from the University of Münster. His dissertation on the Heideggerian critique of theological methodologies provided a foundation for his later reflections on hermeneutics and religion. Active in higher education since 1968, he has taught in Illinois, North Carolina, Kentucky, and Texas, giving courses in philosophy, Scripture, world religions, spirituality, and theology. His present position at Oblate School of Theology in San Antonio involves, at levels from undergraduate to doctoral, the preparation of men and women for various ministries, both clerical and lay. His other professional activities have included hospital ministry and spiritual direction. These experiences are essential to his philosophical and theological understanding of personal and communal faith. His post-doctoral study of psychology is reflected in his journal articles and recent research, which deal with psychological interpretations of Scripture. His ecumenical interests are evident in his recent book, *Companions in Consciousness: The Bible and the New Age Movement* (Triumph™ Books, 1994). He is married and has six children in high school and college.